JO VERSO'S
WORLD OF
Cross Stitch

Flowers, Plants and Fishes
Beasts, Birds, Flyes, and Bees
Hills, Dales, Plains and Pastures
Skies, Seas, Rivers, Trees.
There's nothing near at hand or farthest sought
But with the needle may be shap'd and wrought.

John Taylor, from *The Needle's Excellency,*
        a seventeenth-century pattern book.

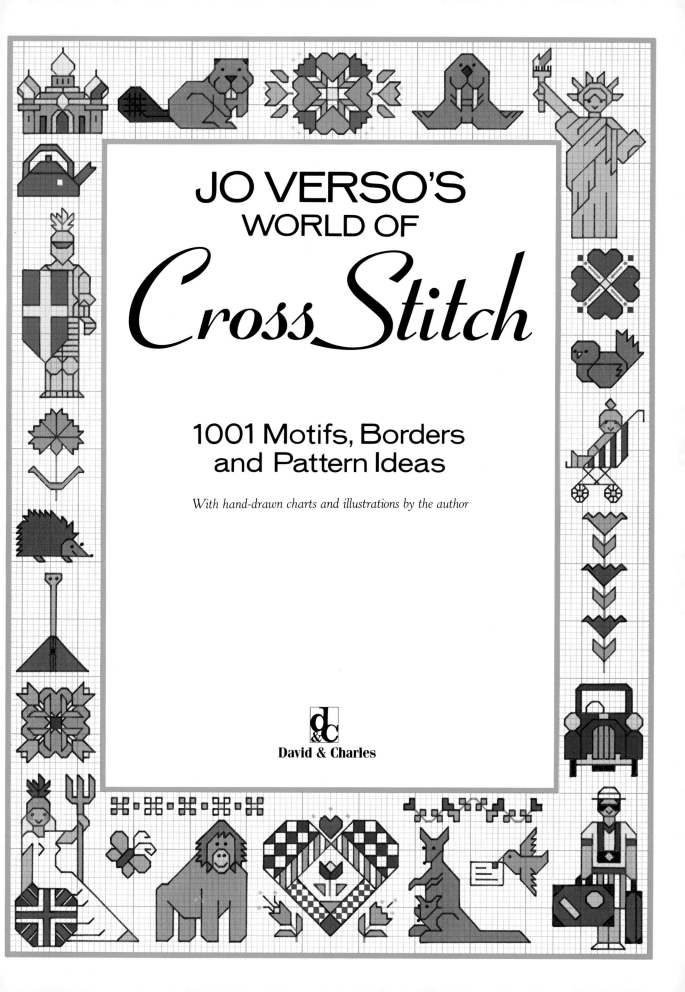

JO VERSO'S
WORLD OF
Cross Stitch

1001 Motifs, Borders and Pattern Ideas

With hand-drawn charts and illustrations by the author

d&c
David & Charles

To my daughters,
Nancy and Amy,
who mean
the world
to me

A DAVID & CHARLES BOOK

Copyright © Jo Verso, 1992
Photography by Di Lewis, except p81 by Alan Duns
First published 1992
Reprinted 1992 (twice), 1993 (twice), 1994 (twice)

Jo Verso has asserted her right to be identified
as author of this work in accordance with the Copyright, Designs
and Patents Act 1988.

A catalogue record for this book is available from the British
Library.

Typeset by ICON, Exeter
and printed in Italy
by LEGO SpA, Vicenza
for David & Charles
Brunel House Newton Abbot Devon

Contents

Introduction

My first book, *Picture It in Cross Stitch*, was published in 1988. The aim of the book was to take the mystery and terror out of designing for cross stitch embroidery, and so to encourage embroiderers to create their own personalised designs. A selection of contemporary patterns was offered, so that samplers and other projects could be worked which reflect life in the late twentieth century. The intention was to provide interest not only for the embroiderer working the project, but hopefully for future generations as well. Such topical and personal embroideries are usually treasured and handed down through generations of a family. Just as an eighteenth-century sampler gives us a glimpse into life as it was lived then, so these embroideries will tell our descendants much about the way we are living now.

Many people doubt their own artistic abilities and find the prospect of drawing and designing too daunting even to contemplate. Judging by the number of letters and photographs of finished projects which readers have been kind enough to send me, the book enabled many cross stitch embroiderers to branch out into producing their own designs. The pleasure and satisfaction that this has afforded them has been obvious, and there have been many requests for more patterns in the same vein.

This book is therefore intended to be a further source of design ideas, and expands the material in *Picture It in Cross Stitch* to cover a much wider field. Domestic life is catered for with a large variety of brand new patterns, so that life at home can be recorded. A 'round-the-world' section has been added for those who want to look further afield, to record their travels, or who have family and friends abroad. Designs of life in the past are included so that history buffs can have their interests recorded on samplers or keepsakes. Also provided are other useful designs such as alphabets and numbers, borders, and spot motifs to fill any awkward gaps.

If you are not an experienced embroiderer, then cross stitch is an ideal introduction to the craft. Providing you can count stitches accurately from a chart and you can keep your stitching neat, a successful result is guaranteed. Having mastered cross stitch, you may then gain the confidence to express yourself in other forms of embroidery. Many people, however, find cross stitch embroidery addictive.

Perhaps you have never designed before and are daunted at the thought of wrestling with graph paper and pencil. The design process is explained clearly, step by step, and will enable you to undertake your chosen project with confidence. Or perhaps you have worked kits and would now like to try your hand at something more personal and adventurous. Here you will find all the ingredients to design your own patterns, together with photographs to show you some of the uses to which the designs can be put.

Instructions on mounting the finished work are given briefly, to allow as much room as possible for design material. Most of your projects will simply need to be framed, and this can be undertaken by a professional framer. Basic needlework skills and the use of glue and card will take care of other projects.

Colour keys are not provided, again to leave as much space as possible for designs, and to allow you personal choice and expression in this area as well. The colour charts show at a glance how the finished embroidery will look, but the method by which the charts are produced does not allow for the use of subtle shades. If the colours are too bright for your taste, remember that much subtler shades are available in the stranded cottons used for the embroidery. The colour photographs can be used as a guide if you particularly want to match the illustrated samples.

Stitching instructions are given, for no matter how good the design it is no use if you cannot stitch it accurately onto the fabric. For beginners it is strongly recommended that the three-quarter cross stitch, an essential part of most of these designs, is fully mastered on spare fabric before starting to work a project.

Some patterns can be stitched straight off the page, but mostly you will select and re-group the designs that you want – and, of course, the permutations are endless. Select them to make your own unique pattern and hence your own record of life or personalised gift. The patterns in all my books are designed on a mix-and-match basis, so be adventurous, choosing and combining those designs that suit your purpose.

A project can be as big or as small as you like – the choice of size and content are yours, as is the world of creativity and fun that hopefully this book will provide.

Plate 1 Design materials ▷

6

Design Your Own Sampler

Cross stitch embroidery is worked from a pattern which is drawn onto graph paper.

A full cross stitch forms a square shape when stitched; a three-quarter cross stitch forms a right-angled triangle. Your design must therefore consist solely of these two shapes or it will be unstitchable (Fig 1).

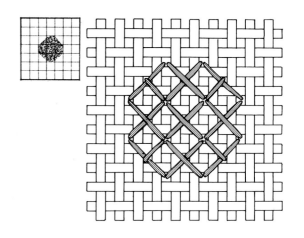

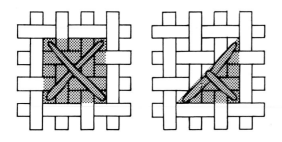

Fig 3 Each right-angled triangle on the chart becomes one three-quarter cross stitch on the fabric

Fig 1 A full cross stitch forms a square shape when sewn; a three-quarter cross stitch forms a right-angled triangle

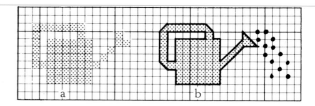

Fig 4a A small watering can, designed using full cross stitch alone, and Fig 4b, a more recognisable watering can, designed with the addition of three-quarter cross stitch, back stitch and French knots

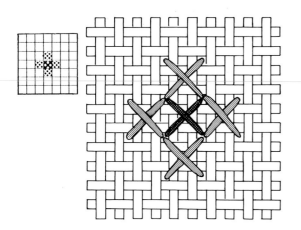

Fig 2 One full square on the chart becomes one full cross stitch on the fabric

* Each filled square on the graph paper will then be worked as a full cross stitch on the fabric (Fig 2).
* Each filled right-angled triangle will be worked as a three-quarter cross stitch (Fig 3). When full squares are combined with right-angled triangles, it is possible to achieve a more naturalistic look (Figs 4a & b).
* Dots will be worked as French knots and drawn lines will be worked in back stitch (Fig 5).
* Empty spaces are left as bare fabric because the background is not worked in cross stitch embroidery.

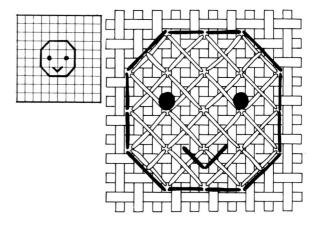

Fig 5 Full cross stitch, three-quarter cross stitch, back stitch and French knots worked on evenweave fabric

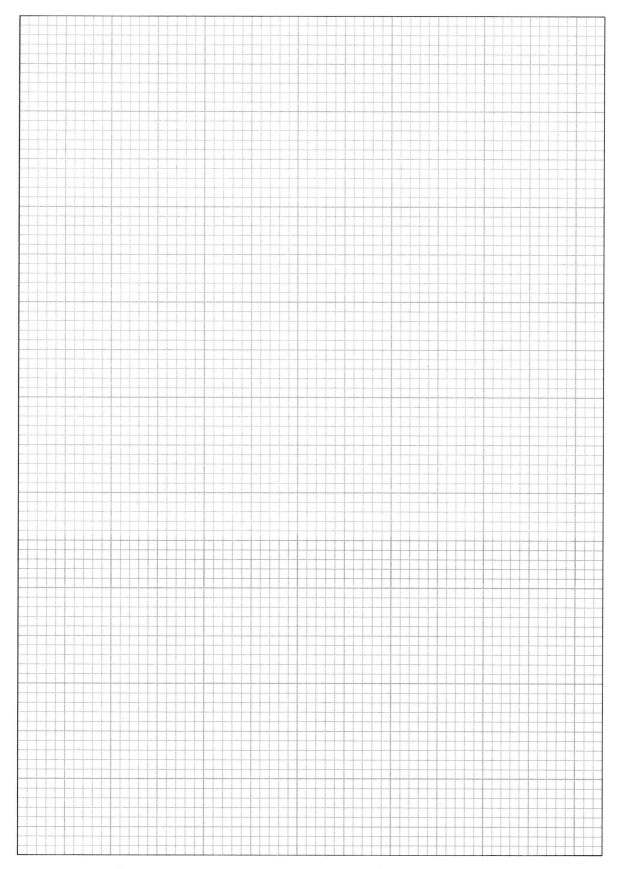

Fig 6 Graph paper

✠ *Design your own Sampler* ✠

Plate 2 Listing, then drawing designs onto graph paper

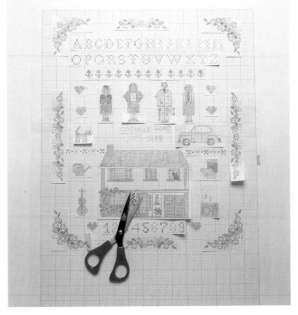

Plate 3 Cutting out, then arranging designs on a master sheet

You will need graph paper large enough for the finished design (the master sheet) and spare graph paper onto which the components of the design will be drawn. Graph paper which has 10 squares to 1in (2.5cm) is ideal. It can be bought in pads or as large, loose sheets. A sheet of such graph paper (Fig 6, p9) has been provided for you to photocopy. Small sheets can be glued together to make larger sheets, taking care to line up the squares accurately at the join.

Step 1 First make a list of everything you would like to include in your sampler. When designing the sampler in Plate 6 my list read as follows:
* a butterfly border
* an alphabet
* numbers
* my house
* myself
* my husband
* my daughters, Nancy and Amy
* the cat
* my Morris Minor
* Nancy's music
* Amy's violin
* my two books
* my husband's interest in gardening (a watering can)
* hearts and flowers to fill any gaps (fillers)
* location and dates

Step 2 Copy out each design on the list onto graph paper using a pencil. Colour in each design using coloured crayons (Plate 2). Cut out each design leaving one clear square all round. Use paper-cutting scissors to avoid blunting your embroidery scissors. As you work, keep the design slips safely in an envelope to prevent them straying and ending up in the vacuum cleaner.

When all the items on your list have been copied, coloured and cut out, start to lay the slips onto the master sheet and begin to build up a first design (Plate 3).

Step 3 Shuffle the slips around on the master sheet until you achieve a pleasing, balanced design. Because you have not drawn directly onto the master sheet, you can try out many different combinations of the material without having to erase and re-draw every time you change your mind. This saves a lot of time and avoids a great deal of irritation.

Step 4 When you are satisfied with your arrangement of all the slips, stick them to the master sheet using adhesive (Plate 4). A non-permanent adhesive, such as Pelikan Roll-fix, allows you to reposition the slips several times.

Take care to align the squares on the slips with the lines on the master sheet.

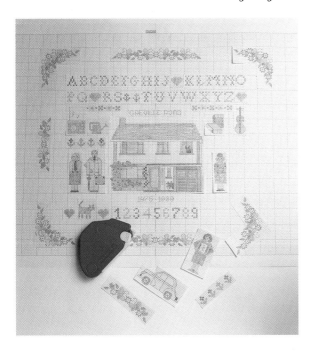

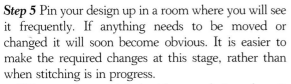

Plate 4 Re-arranging to get a better result, then sticking designs to the master sheet

Plate 5 The finished design

Step 5 Pin your design up in a room where you will see it frequently. If anything needs to be moved or changed it will soon become obvious. It is easier to make the required changes at this stage, rather than when stitching is in progress.

When you are satisfied with your design, draw it out again onto another master sheet which will serve as your pattern for stitching (Plate 5). It is tempting to work from your first master sheet, but the non-permanent glue might allow slips to come adrift and get lost during stitching.

This five-step process can be used not only for designing samplers but also for any other project where you choose to combine different designs.

YOUR QUESTIONS ANSWERED

* What do I do if an item on my list does not appear in the book for me to copy?
* If you cannot draw the item yourself, or if you fail to find the design you need in this or other books, then tracing paper will come to the rescue. Find an illustration of the item; useful sources can be catalogues, photographs, postcards or your local library. Children's books are invaluable for simple line drawings, and my librarian has always been happy to help me find any illustration needed.

Trace the illustration onto graph paper and square-up the design to make a pattern (Fig 7 overleaf). Draw closely to the original lines, but remember you can only use full squares or right-angled triangles. Erase the original line to show a stitchable pattern.

For a short cut, use either tracing graph paper or clear, graphed acetate sheets called Easy Grid (for a supplier of both, see p126). These can be laid over an illustration (Fig 8 overleaf), which can then be squared-up as you trace. Use a pencil on tracing graph paper and a felt-tip pen which will wipe off if you use Easy Grid. Then simply transfer the design onto the graph paper that you are using for the rest of the work.

* How do I square-up a line which rises neither vertically nor at an obliging angle of 45°?
* Off-setting is a useful technique when squaring-up items like church steeples. It reduces the very 'stepped' effect that results when three-quarter cross stitch cannot be used.

Fig 9 overleaf shows the top row of cross stitches off-set by one thread on the fabric (half a square on the chart). Where more than one cross stitch is involved, take care to offset the whole row, not leaving a half stitch at the end of the row which will be unstitchable. An example of the technique can be seen on the top of the Roman soldier's helmet (p44) and on the top of the head-dress on the Statue of Liberty (p99).

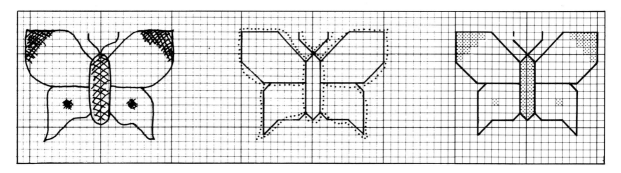

Fig 7 Squaring-up an illustration to make a pattern for cross stitch embroidery

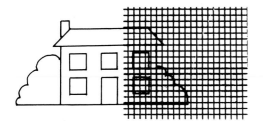

Fig 8 Tracing graph paper or Easy Grid can be laid over an illustration to simplify the squaring-up process

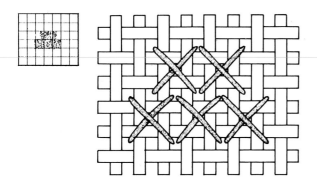

Fig 9 Off-setting a row of full cross stitches by one thread (half a square on the chart)

* *How do I enlarge or reduce an illustration that I want to chart?*
* If the illustration you wish to use is the wrong size to match the rest of your design, you will need access to a modern photocopier. These machines can enlarge or reduce a line drawing at minimal cost, and can be found at your local high street printers. You can then proceed to square-up the design as described above. Allow yourself some artistic licence, and reduce very fiddly designs to the bare essentials.

* *How do I cope with making a pattern of my house or another building?*
* Houses and buildings consist mostly of straight lines. If confident, you can draw your house directly onto graph paper, taking care to get the proportions right. Start with the smallest detail that you want to record, perhaps a small window or other decorative feature. Build the house up around this. Check the size and spacing of the windows and doors. Add the outer walls, ground line and roof. Finally, include any details that will make it look like home, a windowbox perhaps, or your cat at the window.

Too daunting? Tracing graph paper or Easy Grid make the job easier if they are placed over a sketch or photograph of the house. If the photograph is too small or too large, take a tracing of it and have it enlarged or reduced to the desired size.

* *How do I know if my design is well balanced?*
* If you want to follow general rules, keep large items (houses, for example) in the middle and about two-thirds of the way down the design. It is better to be bottom heavy than top heavy. Arrange the rest of your material around the central focal point, distributing it evenly either side. Check that designs are evenly spaced away from the border. Alphabets and numbers, traditionally, are placed at the top and the bottom. Fill any glaring gaps with fillers or spot motifs.

Any design which faces one way – a train, for example – should face inwards so that the eye is drawn into the centre of the design. To reverse a design, hold a small hand mirror alongside it and copy the reflection onto graph paper. The train can then chug into the picture rather than out of it.

Having said all that, because this is *your* design you are free to break the 'rules' in any way you wish. Since this is your own work, it is a reflection of your personality, it is your 'statement'. The best test is to decide if *you* like the design.

Plate 6 The Verso household, stitched and framed ▷

✠ *Borders* ✠

Many designs benefit from the addition of a border to make a 'frame' for all the separate elements included in them. Borders need not be a chore to be ploughed through when the interesting bits have been done: with a little imagination and forethought, they can add even more interest to the piece and reflect the main subject matter in some way. Beware, though, of letting the border 'take over', distract from, or swamp the main design.

* The simplest borders of all are single lines of cross stitches surrounding the design (Plates 14 & 16).
* Wider borders can consist of many separate designs related to the subject matter they are enclosing (Plates 18 & 20).
* A border need not run unbroken around the complete design if extra space is needed to add information which will not fit within the design (Plate 24).
* A border can be stitched separately onto contrasting fabric for extra interest (Plates 6 & 15). The centre is removed from the fabric on which the border has been stitched. The border is then mounted onto card, which is laid over the main picture. If there are two stitchers in your family, one can be working on the border and the other on the main piece, which is a great time saver.
* Bands can be used to create a border, or can be placed with a spot motif in each corner (Fig 10). A modified version of this can be seen in Plate 6.

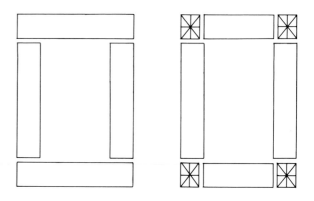

Fig 10 Placement of bands, or bands with symbols in the corners, to form borders

Fig 11 Using a hand mirror to produce a corner from a band

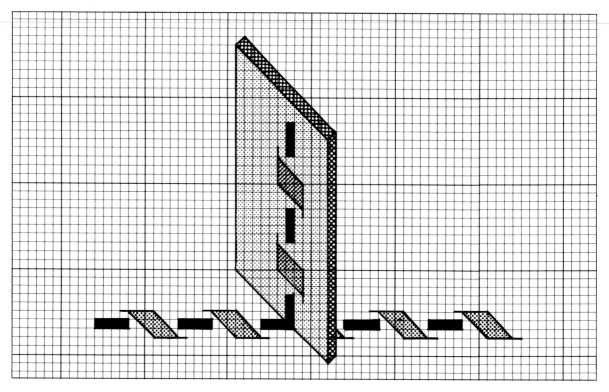

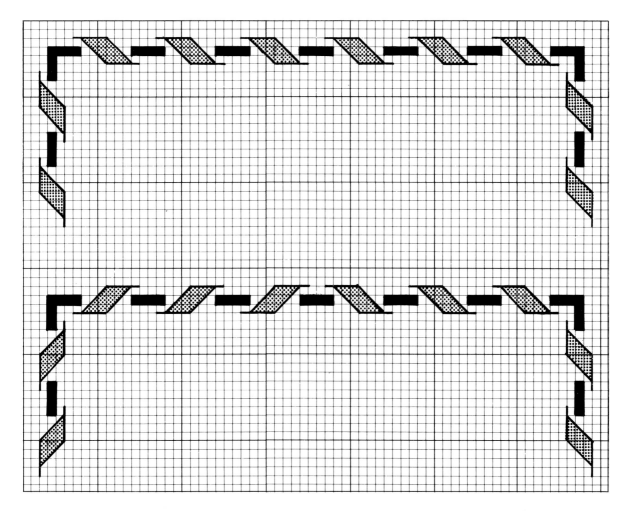

Fig 12 Reversing a pattern that slopes in one direction

* If there is a band which you would like to use as a continuous border, you will have to invent a corner. Place a small hand mirror on the band at an angle of 45° and move it along the band until a pleasing corner is reflected in the mirror (Fig 11). Copy the reflection onto graph paper. This was the method used to design the border in Plate 9.

* Where a pattern repeat slopes in one direction, it may be desirable to break the run at the centre of each side and reverse the pattern at this point to ensure four similar corners (Figs 12 & 13). This was the method used in Plates 15 & 23.

Whatever border you choose, draw out the four corners and sides onto L-shaped strips of graph paper. Fit them around the design on the master sheet, making any adjustments necessary and paying particular attention to the joins.

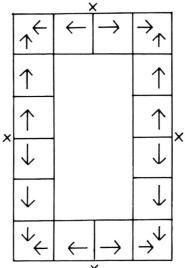

Fig 13 Pattern repeats slope in the direction of the arrows and reversal points at X give the border four similar corners

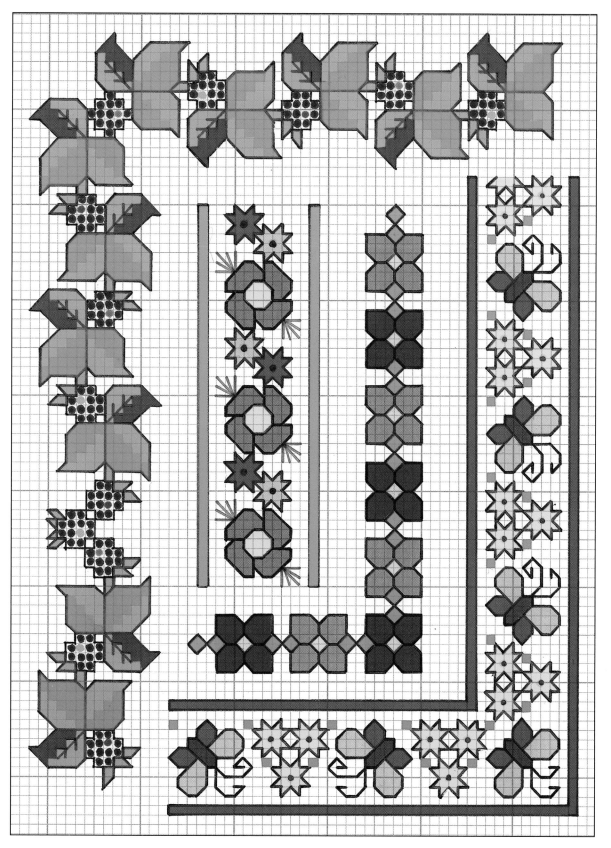

✤ All-over Patterns ✤

A simple all-over pattern makes a good project for a beginner. Use the patterns for pincushions, sachets, (Plate 8), needlecases and so on. The Flora Frame shown here (Plate 7) includes a container for fresh or dried flowers which slots behind the front section. Dismantle the frame, cover the front and back sections with the pattern of your choice, then reassemble the frame and fill it with flowers.

When working the heart-shaped sachet (Plate 7), the lines of cross stitches were substituted with ribbon couched to the surface of the fabric (Fig 14). If less of

this pattern is worked, a small lavender bag can be made (Plate 8).

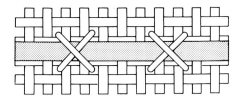

Fig 14 Couching ribbon onto fabric

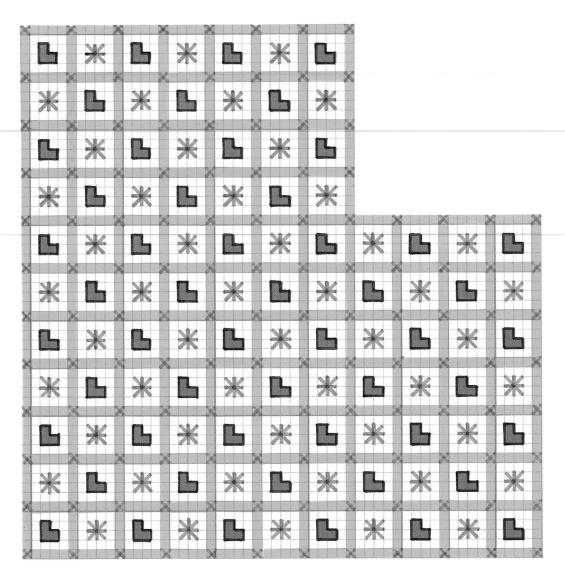

Plate 7 ▷

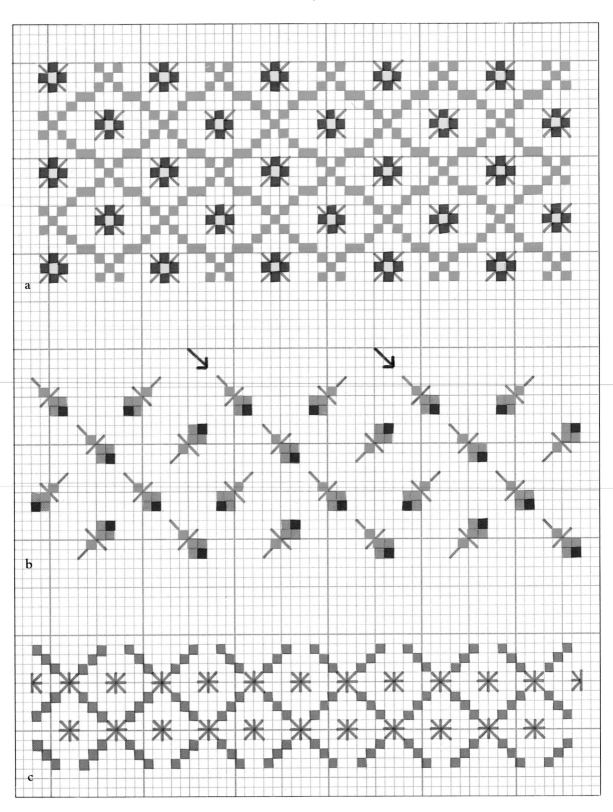

When working pattern (b), simplify the task by first stitching the lines marked with an arrow.

For extra richness, stitch a small sequin in place under the stars in pattern (c) (Plate 26).

Bands

✛ Spot Motifs ✛

On the next two pages you will find a variety of uses
for the patterns in this book.

Plate 8 (overleaf)

23

✚ Fillers ✚

26

✚ *Multi-purpose Patterns* ✚

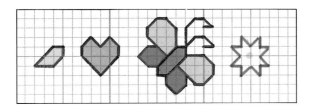

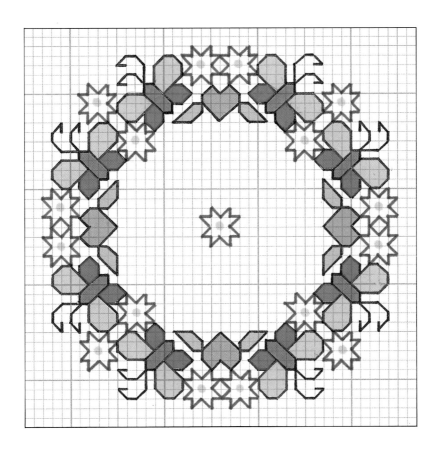

Take a few simple basic ideas – in this case a butterfly, a daisy, a heart and a leaf were chosen – and have fun combining them in many ways to make a multi-purpose pattern. They have been used to design a border (Plate 6), and the dressing table set (Plate 8) consists of just these few basic ingredients placed in different combinations. My initials were added to the centre of the hairbrush and mirror. If the pattern on this page is stitched on Zweigart Linda it will fit the 3¾in (9.5cm) lid of a Framecraft porcelain pot, (Plate 8).

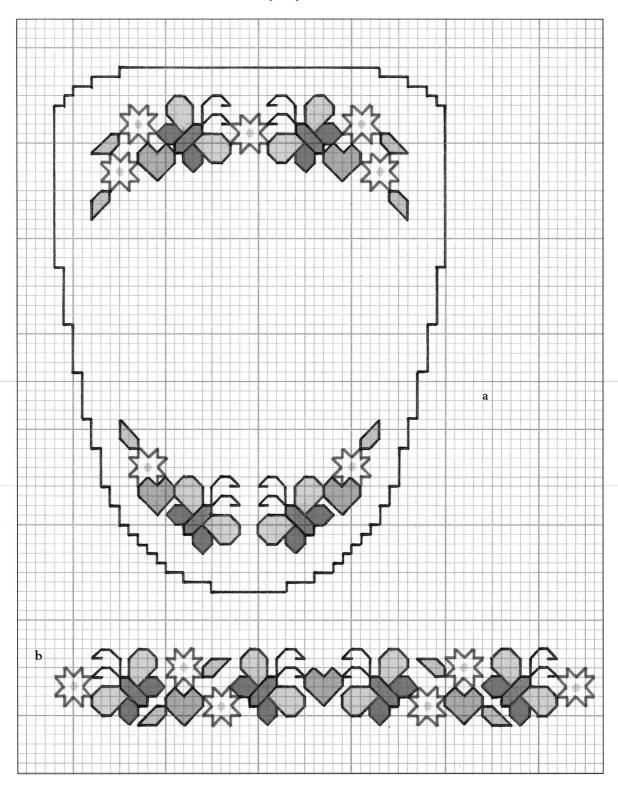

If these three patterns are stitched on Zweigart Linda
they will fit a Framecraft hairbrush (a), clothes brush
(b) and mirror (c), (Plate 8).

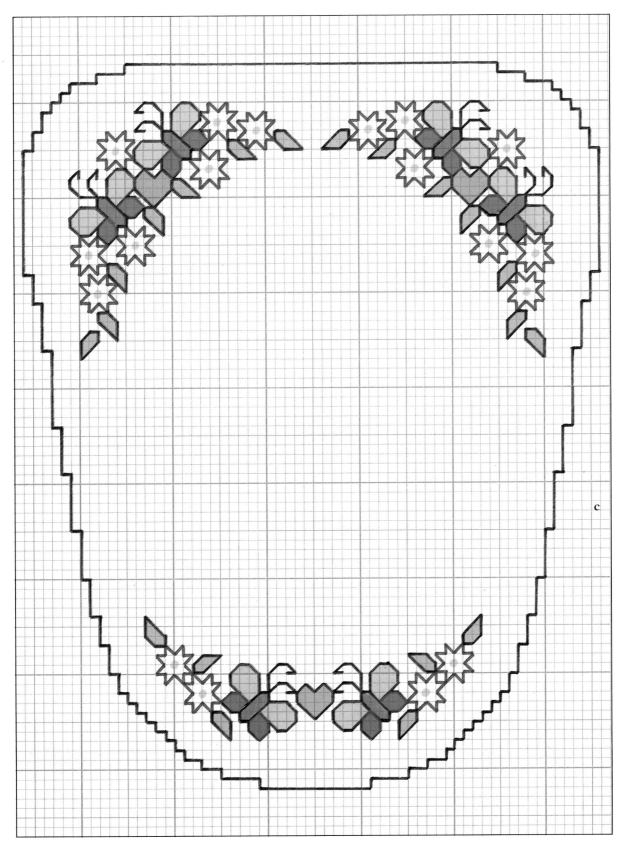

c

✛ *Birth Announcement* ✛

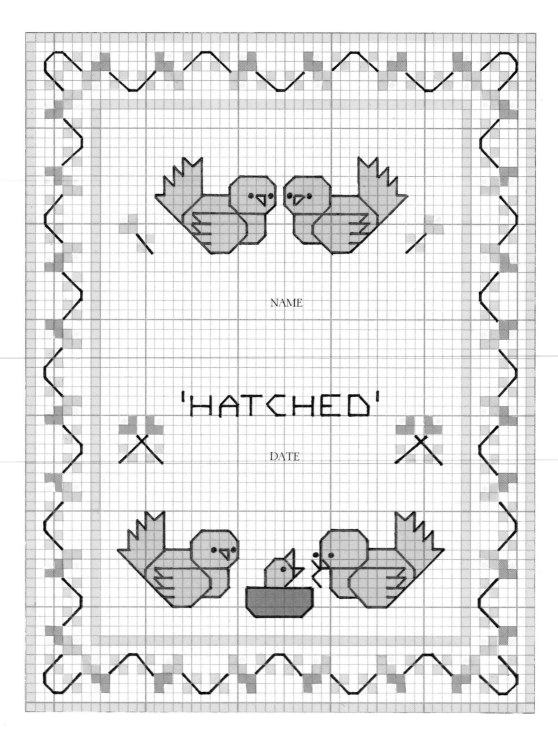

This birth announcement for a Valentine's Day baby was put together using designs from the following sections: Animals, Alphabets and Numbers (Fig 16), Fillers and Bands. A corner was invented as described on p15. If your hatchling has a long name which will not fit the space, choose a smaller alphabet. The framed work hangs on a toning picture bow.

Plate 9 ▷

Flowers

✢ Flowers ✢

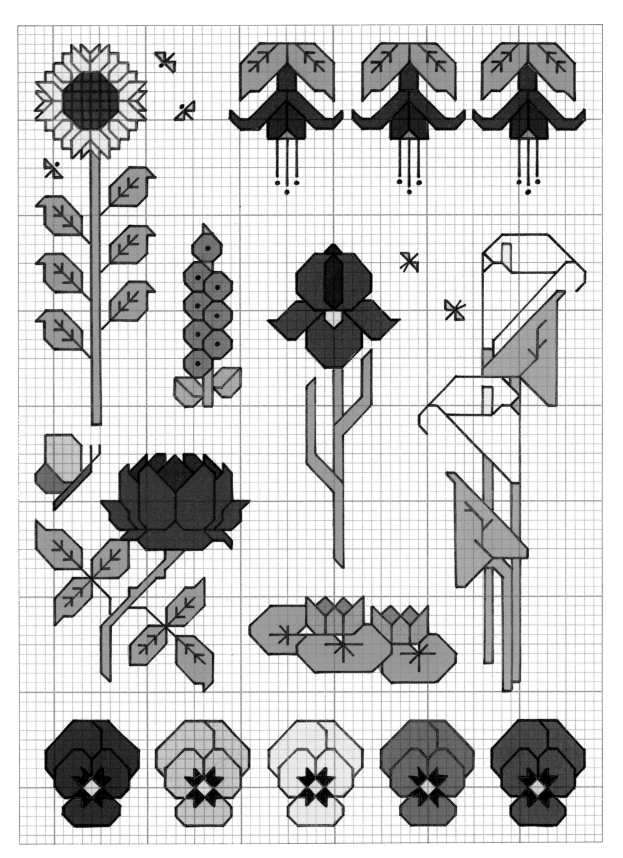

✢ A Favourite Text ✢

The chances are that your favourite text, saying or poem will not be available ready-charted or in kit form. Draw out the lettering on long strips of graph paper, then cut them into lengths and form an attractive arrangement. Finish the design with some appropriate flowers or other motifs. Here, the picture mount echoes the choice of text.

Plate 10 ▷

✤ People ✤

✛ *People* ✛

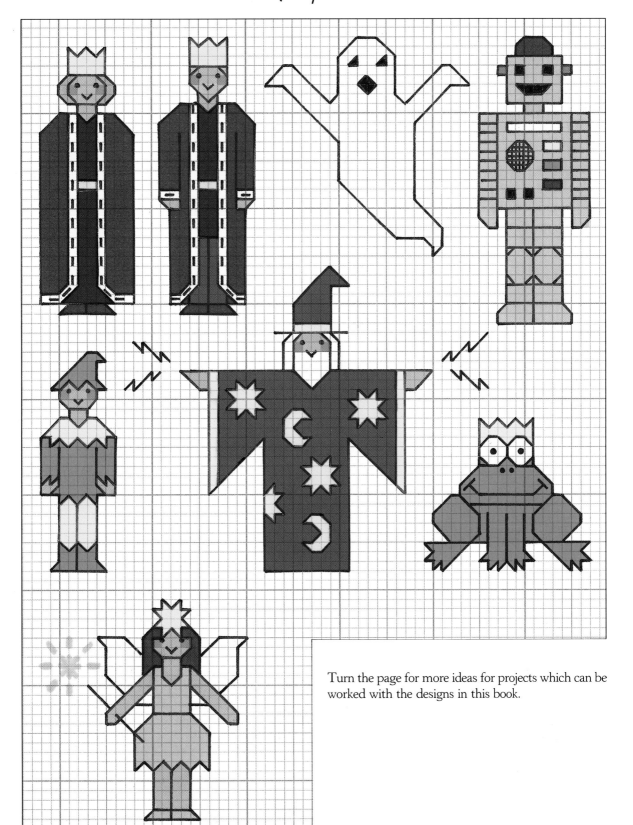

Turn the page for more ideas for projects which can be worked with the designs in this book.

Plate 11 (overleaf)

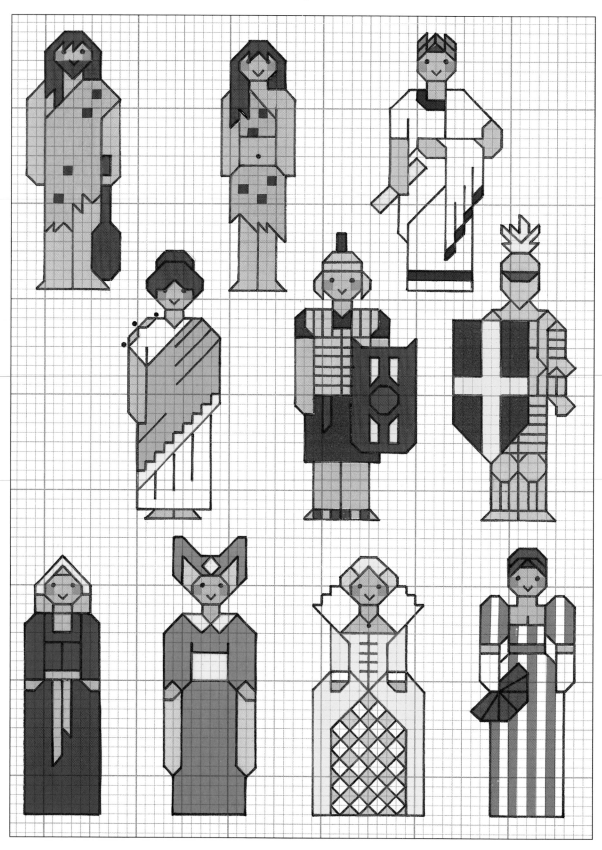

✛ People ✛

✛ Buildings ✛

CRICKET CLUB

THE HALT

SCHOOL

✤ Photograph Album Cover ✤

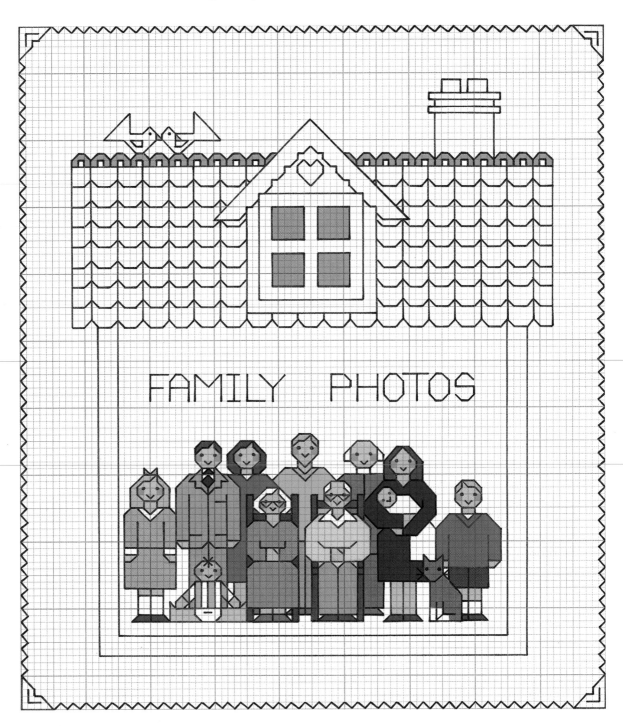

The figures in this design can be replaced with members of your own family for a more personal album cover. Throughout the book you will find many different styles of clothing, headgear, footwear and hairstyles. All are interchangeable and you can create your own character. Take the hairstyle from one figure, the clothing from another, add spectacles if appropriate and a new figure will appear. Cut out each one and overlap them in the available space to make a family group. Finally, add the family name.

Plate 12 ▷

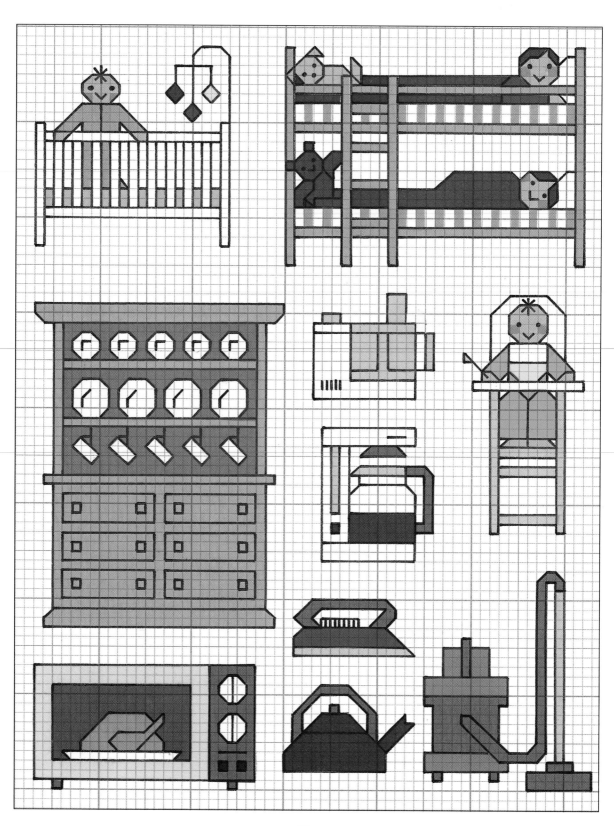

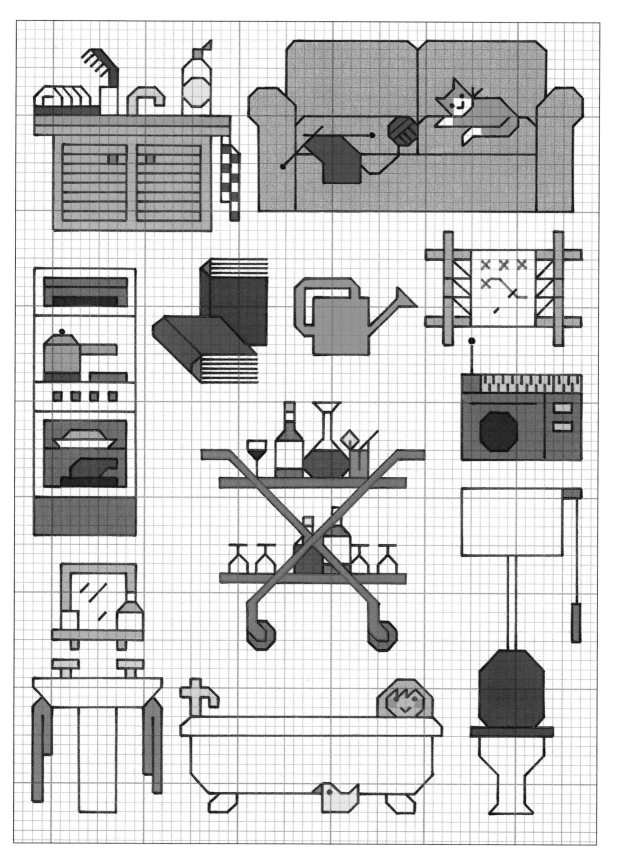

✚ Transport ✚

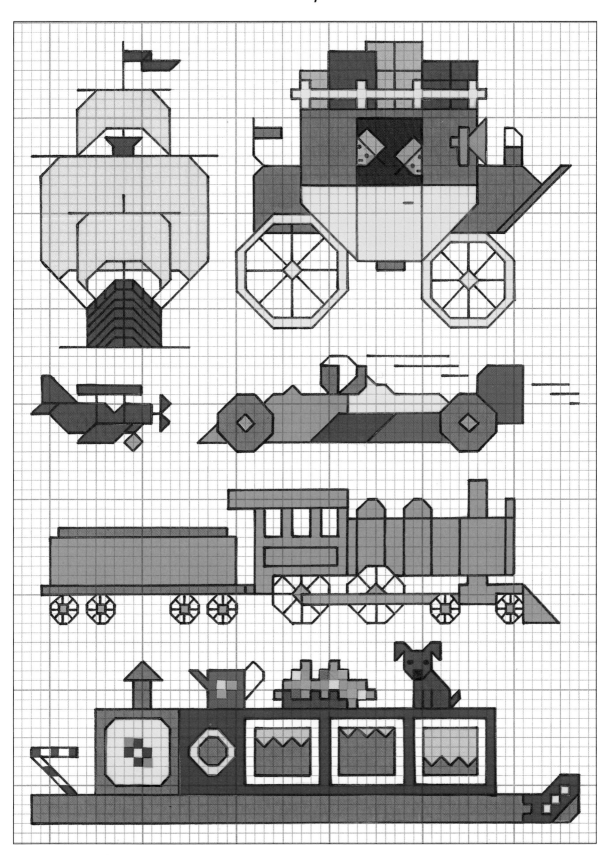

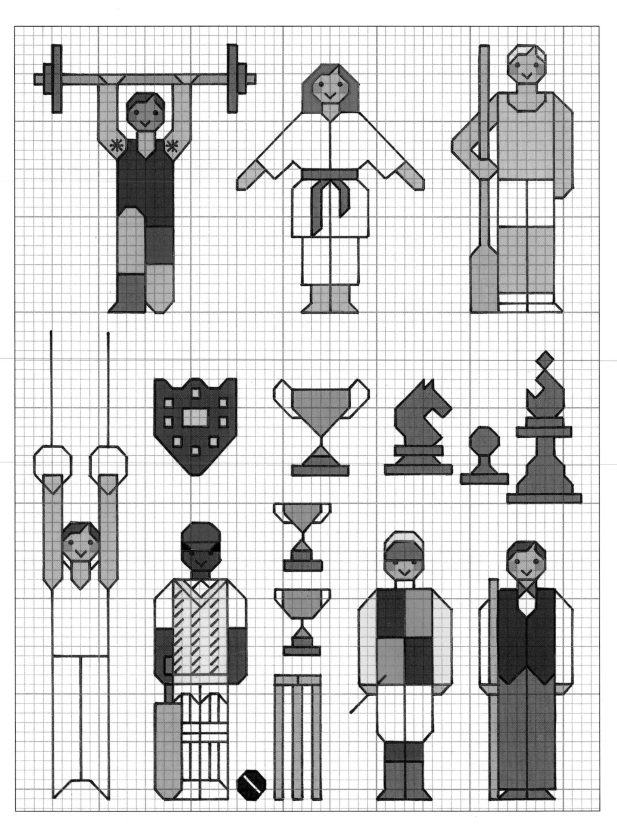

Ask a friendly carpenter to cut a rebate in the back of
an old tennis racquet and use it to frame a record of
sporting achievements.

Plate 13 ▷

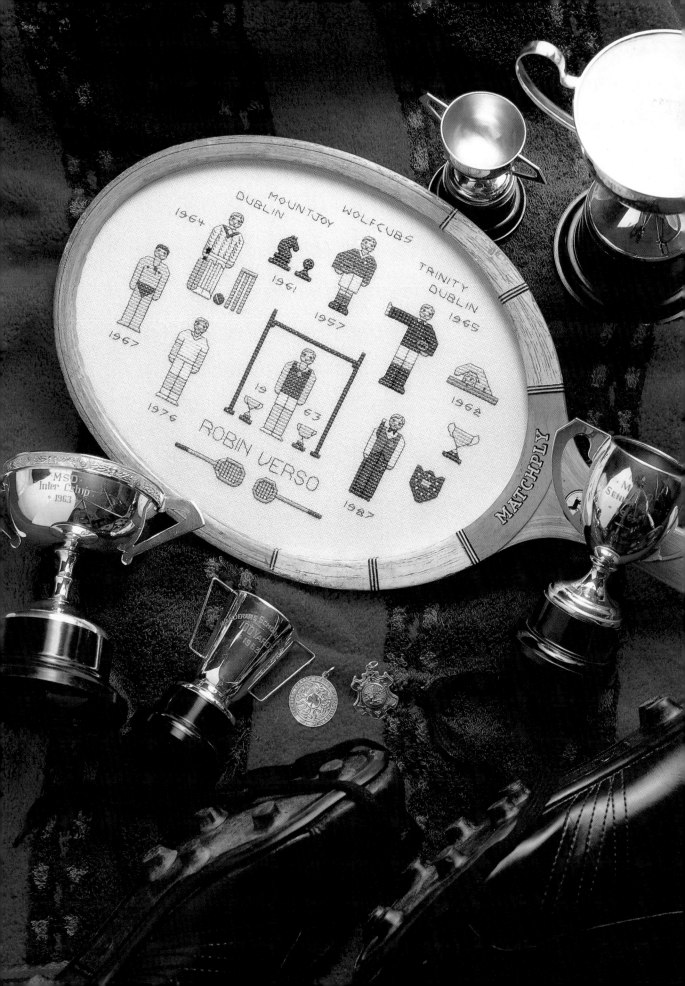

Music

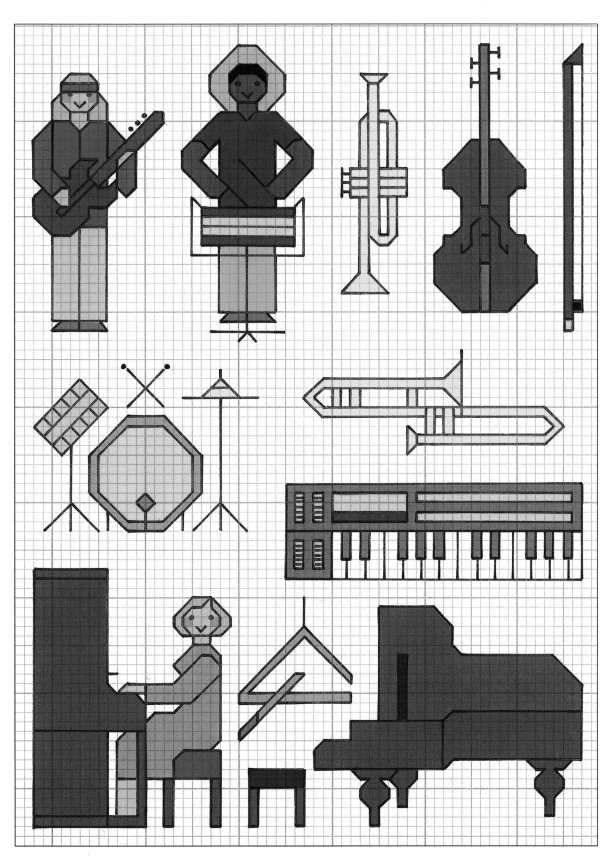

✚ Animals ✚

✠ *Christening Record* ✠

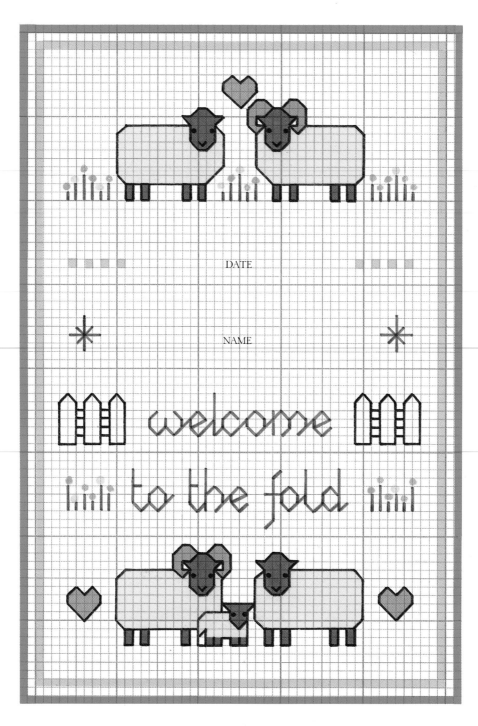

DATE

NAME

welcome

to the fold

This design started with the drawings of the sheep and the lamb. Some fencing from p69 was added, together with some hearts from p27. Lettering and numbers were taken from the Alphabet section; if the name had been longer, a smaller alphabet would have been substituted. Gaps were filled with dots, stars and tiny beaded flowers. The frame chosen for the design is patterned, so the only border needed was a simple line.

Plate 14 ▷

✛ Down on the Farm ✛

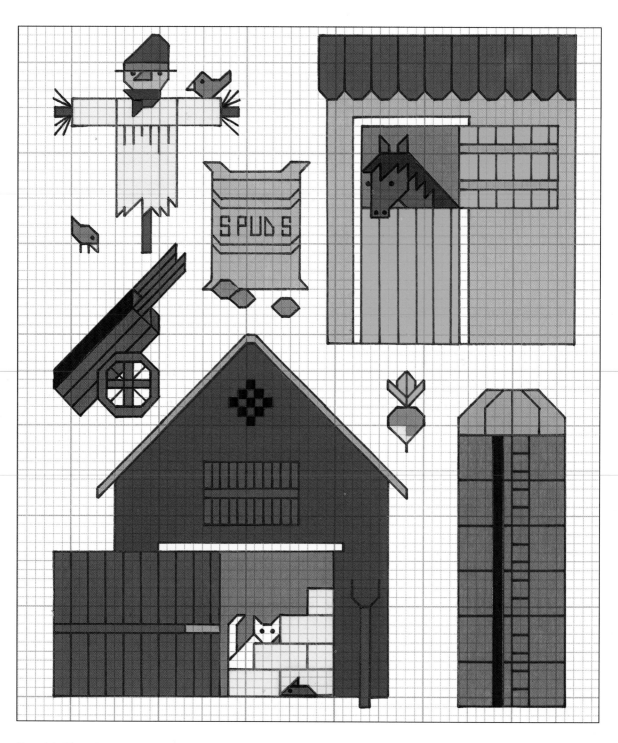

Bramble Farm has been stitched on a cream fabric; the bramble border has been stitched separately onto pale green to form a contrast. To make the blackberries look good enough to eat, a shiny bead has been substituted for each French knot on the chart (p17).

Bramble Farm is an imaginary farm, but maybe the designs in this section will inspire you to re-design along these lines and make a record of an existing farm.

Plate 15 ▷

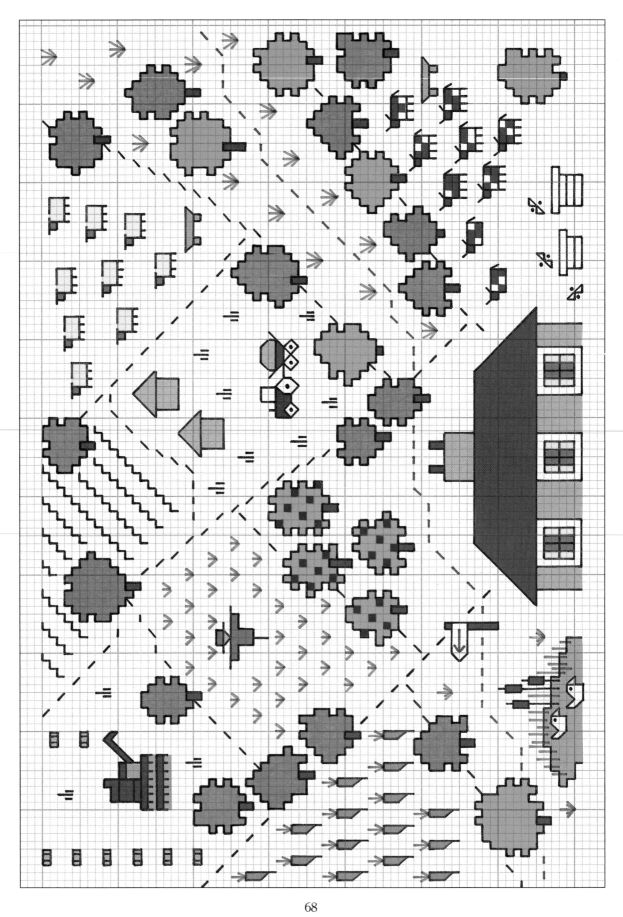

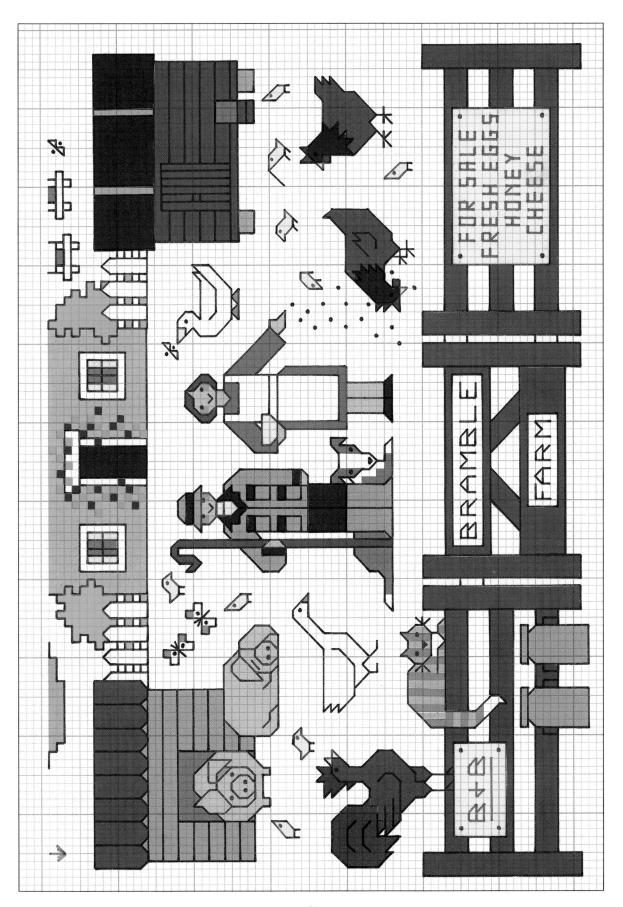

School Days

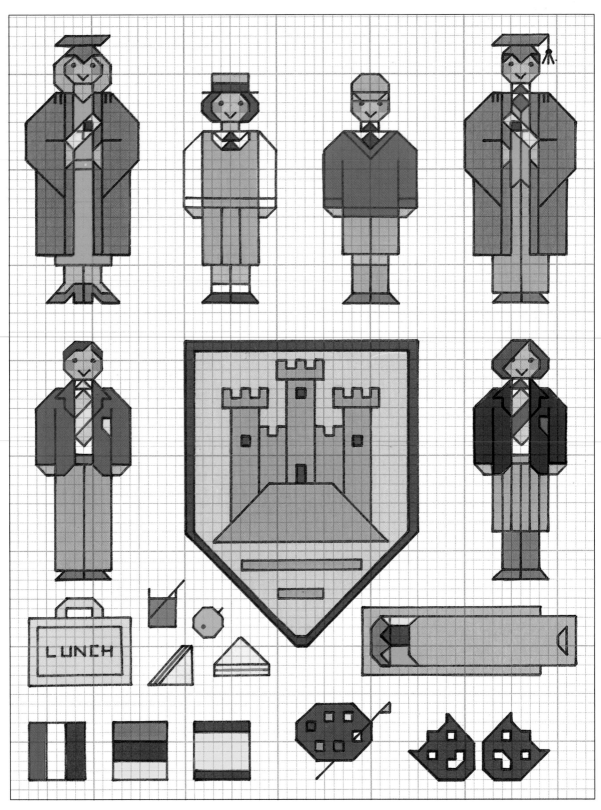

LUNCH

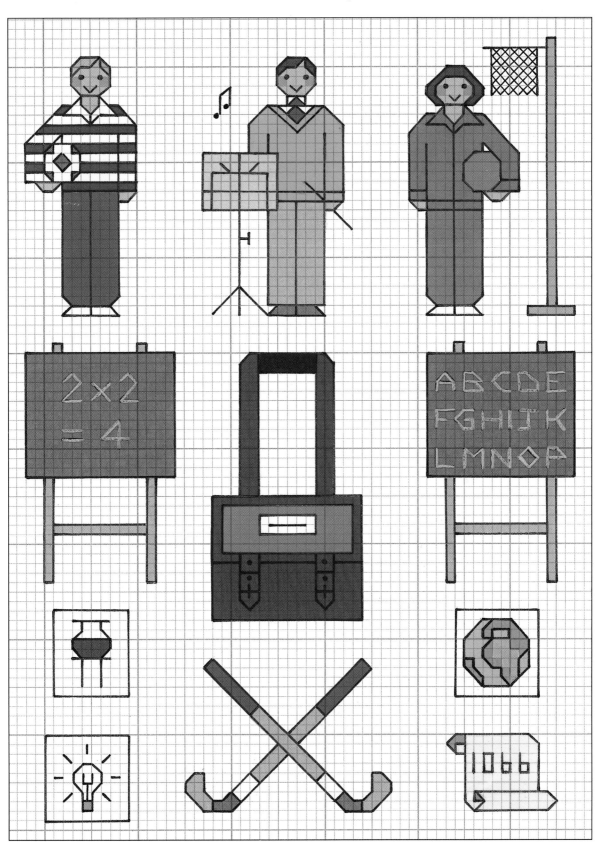

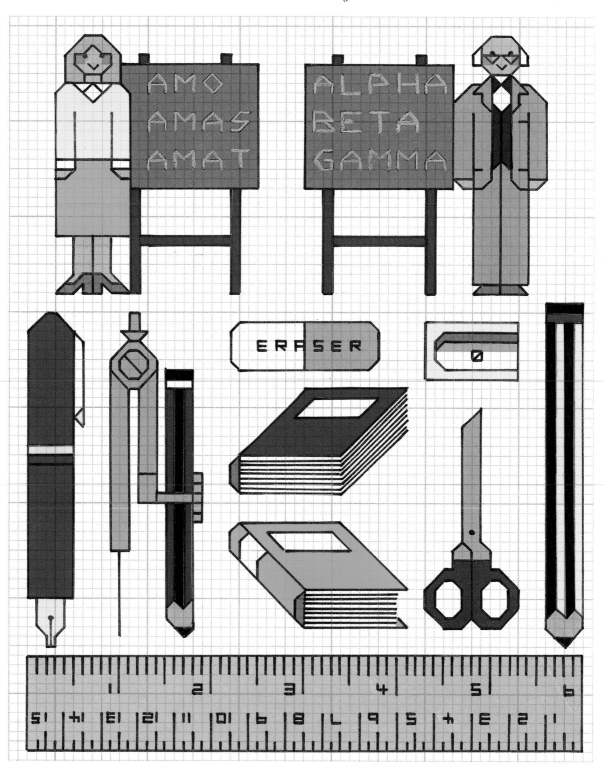

My daughters' school days are recorded here using symbols from the preceding pages. Hairstyles and clothing were adapted to suit the people portrayed and spectacles added by stitching on tiny, metal jewellery jump-rings. An alphabet from the Alphabet section was included to keep the link with traditional sampler-making and to reflect life in the classroom.

Plate 16 ▷

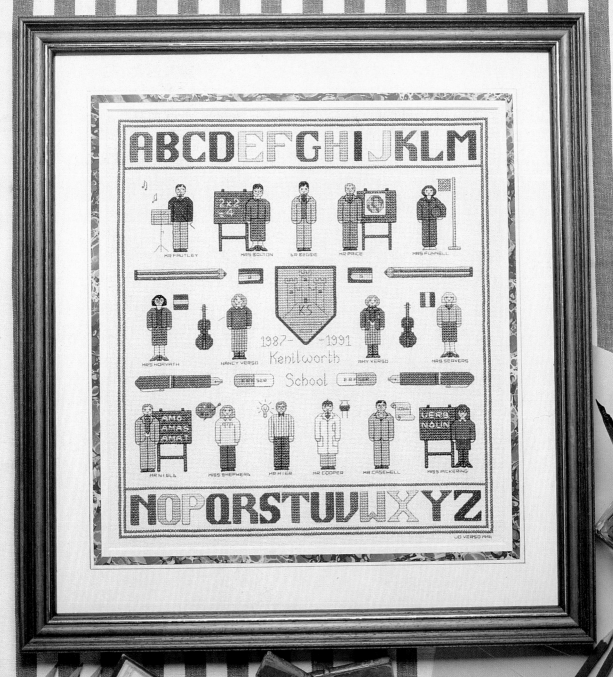

✠ Religious Life ✠

PEACE

--- BE WITH YOU ---

Parish details, the ordination of a priest or other events can be recorded using this design. Just omit the banner and substitute your own lettering. If worked on Zweigart Oslo, or Zweigart Damask Hardanger, this design will fit a Dunlicraft Gothic 9½in (24cm) frame.

Extra masonry can be stitched as indicated on the chart if working on Zweigart 'Oslo' or Damask Hardanger to fit a Dunlicraft Gothic 5½″ × 9½″ (14 × 24cm) frame.

Plate 17 ▷

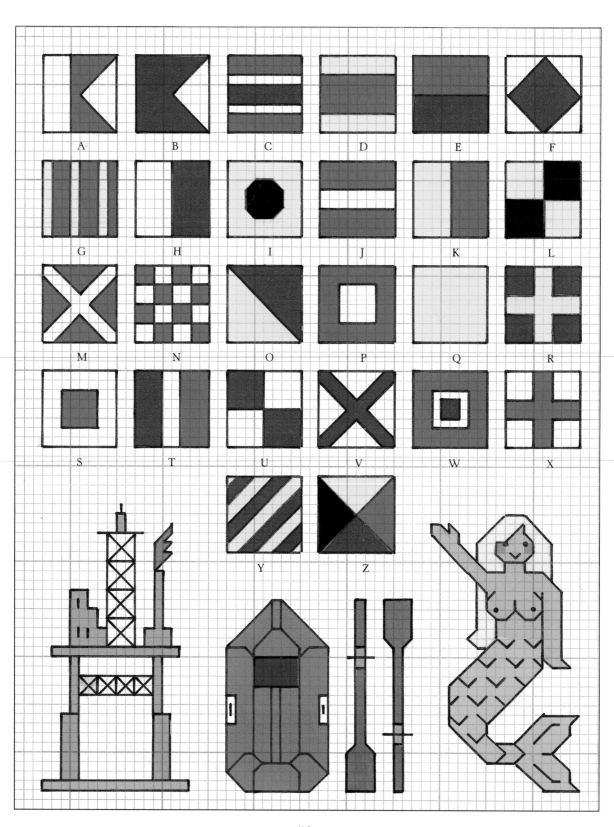

✤ All at Sea ✤

Designs from the preceding pages, together with lettering, have been put together to make a sampler with a nautical theme. The border could consist entirely of the nautical flag alphabet, but here the flags have been used to spell out the names of the embroidress and her partner.

Plate 18 ▷

✠ Around the World in Cross Stitch ✠

This map of the world was a large undertaking, so large in fact that the chart for it could not be reproduced in the book. The finished size of the embroidery is 24½in (62cm) by 18in (46cm). The symbols placed on it appear throughout these pages, so you could trace your own map onto graph paper and add symbols of your choice. If you particularly want to stitch the version in Plate 20, my chart of this work is available separately from The Inglestone Collection (see p127).

The border consists of flags. If a flag does not appear, no disrespect is intended to that country. There was not room to include every flag of the world, and some proved too complicated to reproduce for cross stitch on this small scale. If there is a particular flag that you wish to include in a design, you may find a similar flag that you can adapt (many flags are of similar design which only need a colour change, and as many styles as possible have been included here). Where a flag has a star as part of its design, a star-shaped coloured sequin has been used.

World events have changed since the piece was designed; it was finished in 1991, but work started much earlier. At the time of writing this, at least one flag is obsolete, and others are likely to be replaced. It thus represents a changing world. Sequins have been used to mark the homes of friends, and a 'key' to these was worked in the bottom right-hand corner. Globe-trotters could mark places they have visited with French knots or beads.

Plate 19 Detail of Plate 20 (opposite)

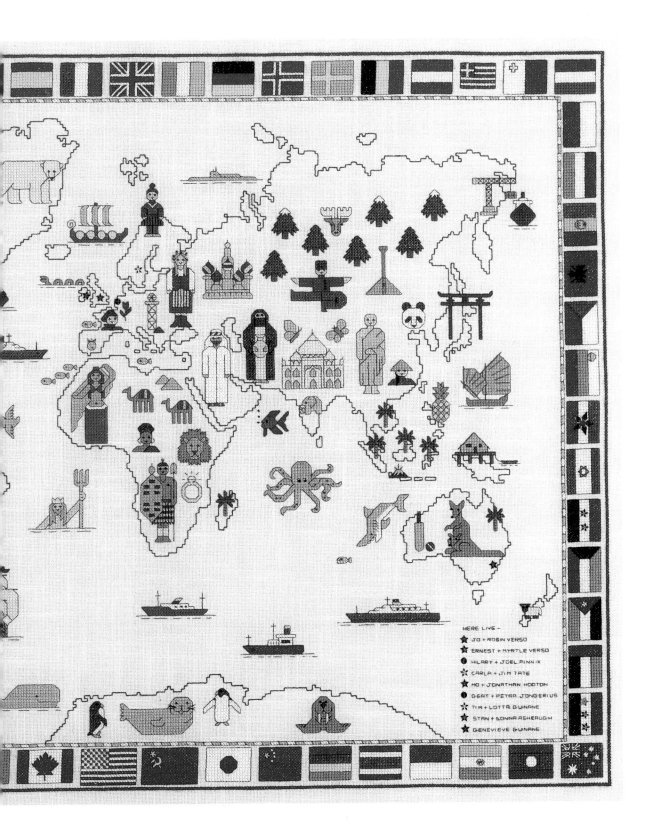

HERE LIVE —

★ JO + ROBIN VERSO
★ ERNEST + MYRTLE VERSO
● HILARY + JOEL PINNIX
✩ CARLA + JIM TATE
◆ MO + JONATHAN HOOTON
● GERT + PETRA JONGERIUS
✰ TIM + LOTTA GUINANE
★ STAN + DONNA ASHBAUGH
★ GENEVIEVE GUINANE

England

United Kingdom

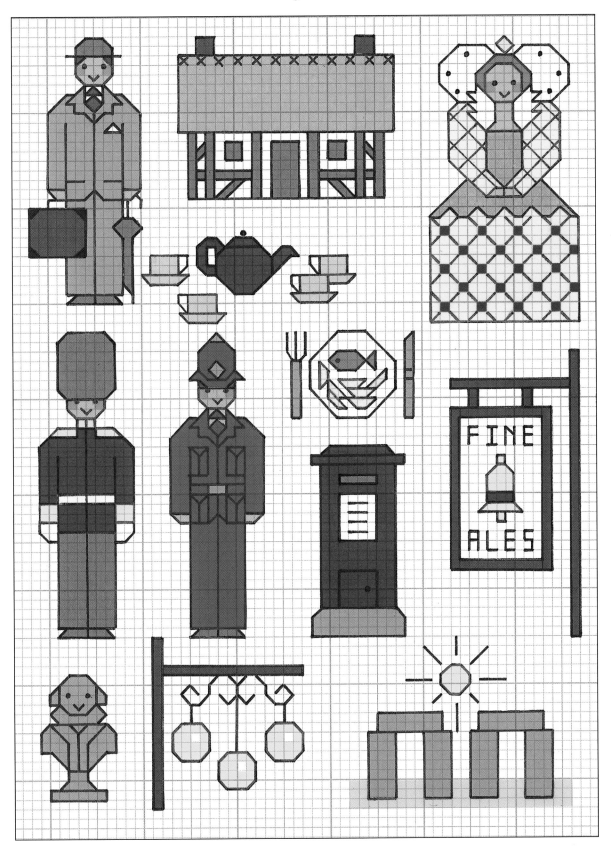

✛ County Map ✛

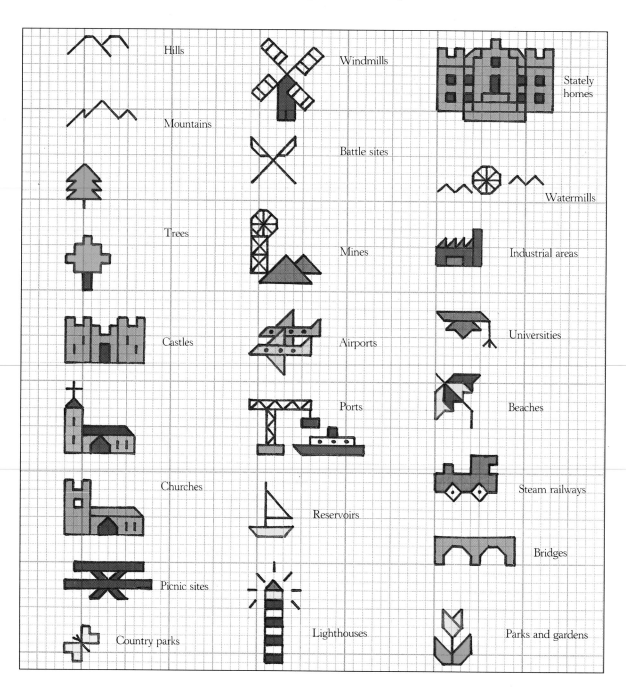

This is my own view of the county where I live. On it have been marked places of particular personal interest, for example, where friends live, places I have visited, and so on.

To make a record of your own county, follow the general instructions given for designing a sampler. Trace the boundary onto a master sheet of graph paper and add rivers and hills. Mark the location of your chosen places of interest. On separate slips, write out town names, copy out appropriate symbols from the selection above, and trees to fill gaps. Position these on the master sheet, then stick the slips into place. Outside the boundary you can add the name of the county, the county badge, a compass, your house or any other appropriate landmark.

Plate 21 ▷

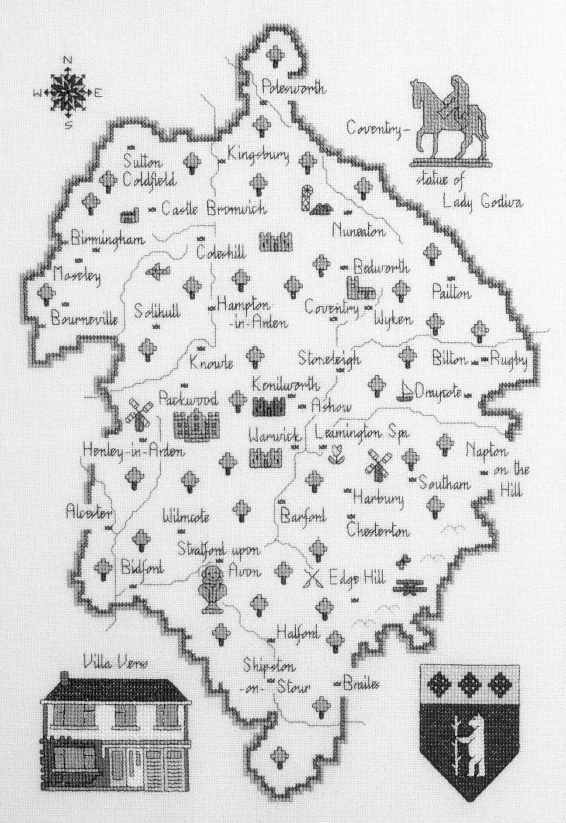

Warwickshire

Scotland

Wales

✛ Ireland ✛

Republic of Ireland

✛ Western Europe ✛

France

Portugal

Spain

✣ Honeymoon Memento ✣

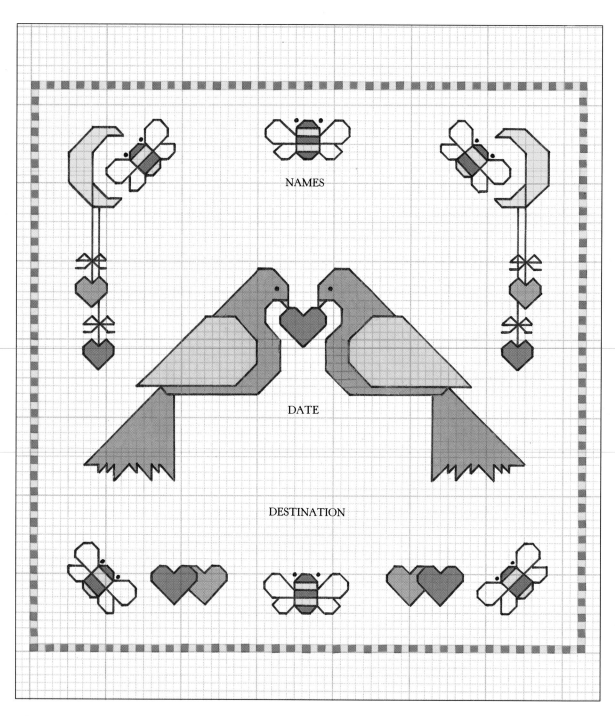

NAMES

DATE

DESTINATION

Honey-bees, moons and lovebirds are incorporated to make a honeymoon memento. The completed work could be framed or, if worked on a fine fabric, mounted as a card to welcome the couple home. The sample shown was worked on Zweigart Shona Damask and then made into a pillow trimmed with lace and ribbon. Space has been left for names, dates and location to be added using an alphabet and numbers from the Alphabet section. You might like to substitute the bee at the bottom with a flag or other symbol suitable to the destination.

Plate 22 ▷

90

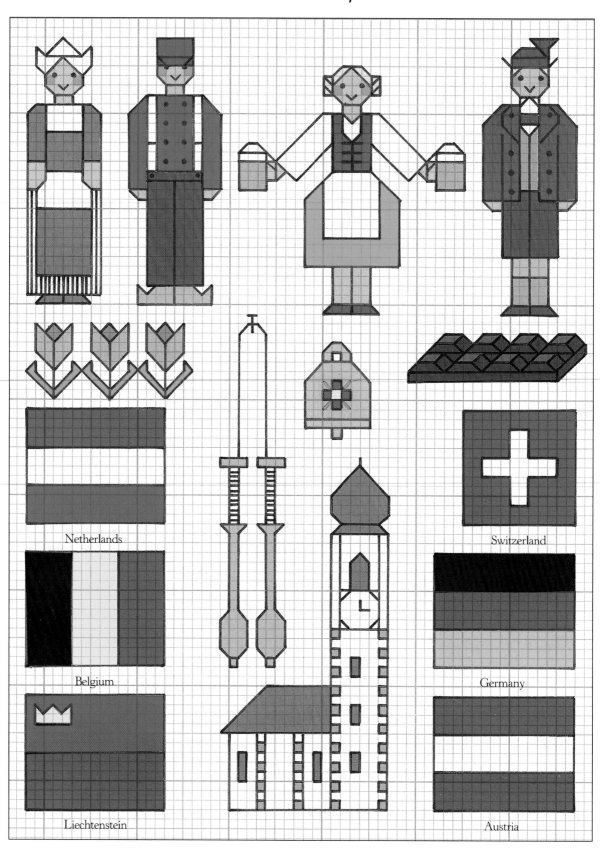

Netherlands

Switzerland

Belgium

Germany

Liechtenstein

Austria

Malta

Italy

Vatican City

San Marino

Monaco

Greece

✤ Scandinavia ✤

Norway

Sweden

Denmark

Finland

A personalised sampler makes a novel thank-you gift for those who have offered you hospitality. This was stitched after a holiday as guests of friends in Sweden, where we stayed in their log-cabin summer house.

Similar samplers can be designed for other countries using the designs in this book.

Plate 23 ▷

✛ Eastern Europe ✛

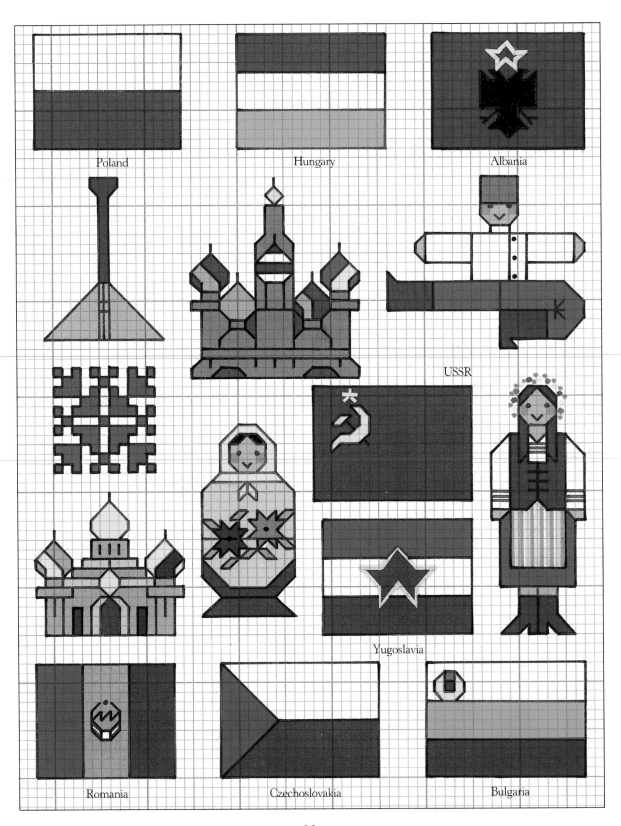

Poland

Hungary

Albania

USSR

Yugoslavia

Romania

Czechoslovakia

Bulgaria

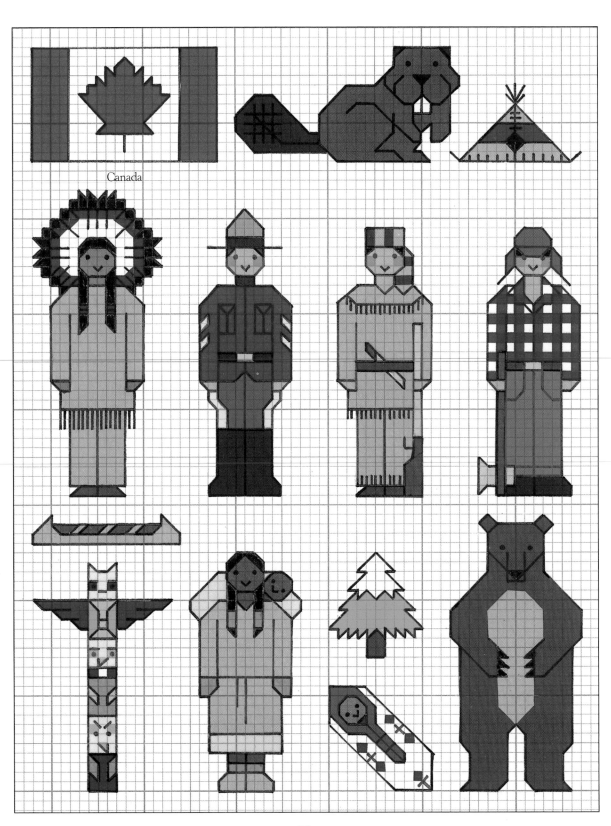

Canada

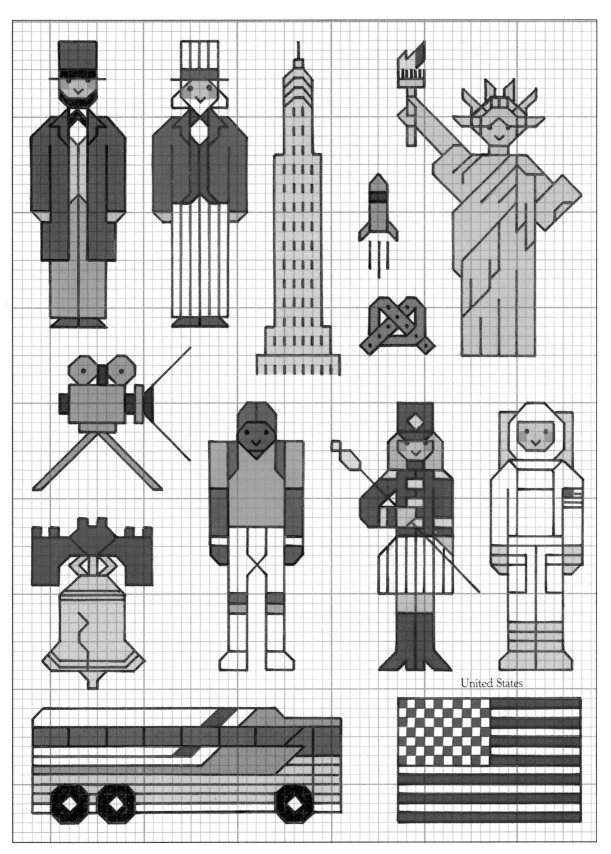

United States

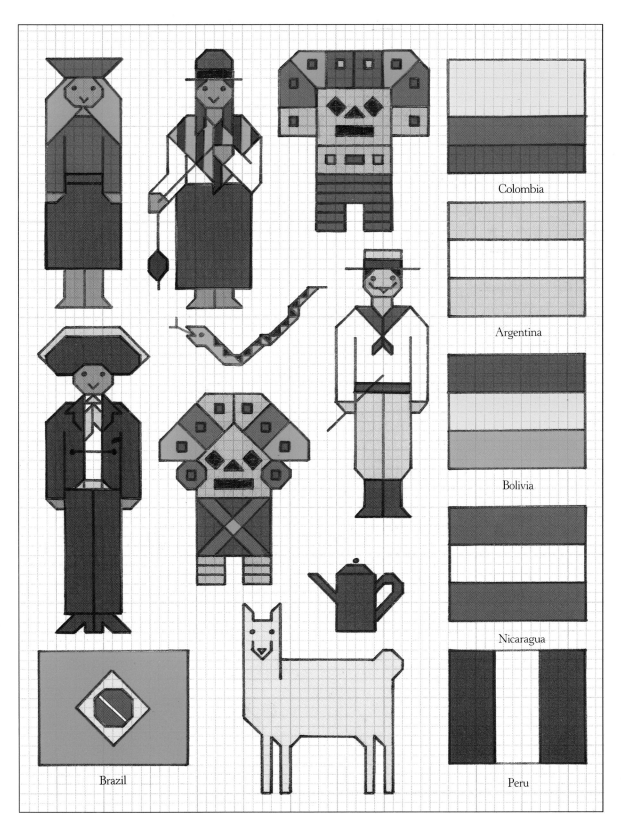

Colombia

Argentina

Bolivia

Nicaragua

Brazil

Peru

✠ Africa ✠

Capture your memories of a special holiday by stitching the local people, animals, buildings and patterns. Draw out symbols for your chosen country, arrange them on a master sheet, separate them with lines of colour and add a suitable border. Here, a holiday in Tunisia has been stitched into a lasting and colourful souvenir.

Plate 24 ▷

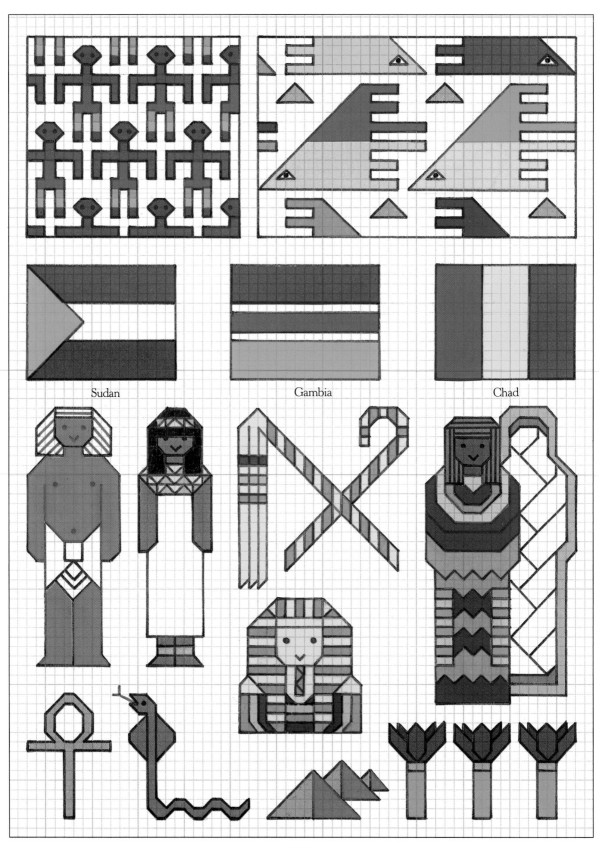

Sudan   Gambia   Chad

Ethiopia

Senegal

Central African Republic

Gabon

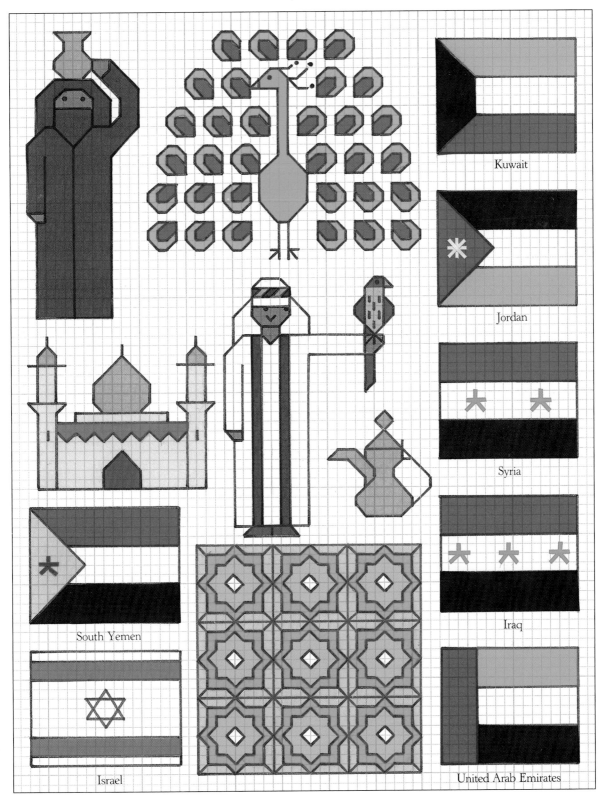

Kuwait

Jordan

Syria

Iraq

South Yemen

Israel

United Arab Emirates

India

Indonesia

Thailand

Bangladesh

Mauritius

Laos

China

Japan

Australasia

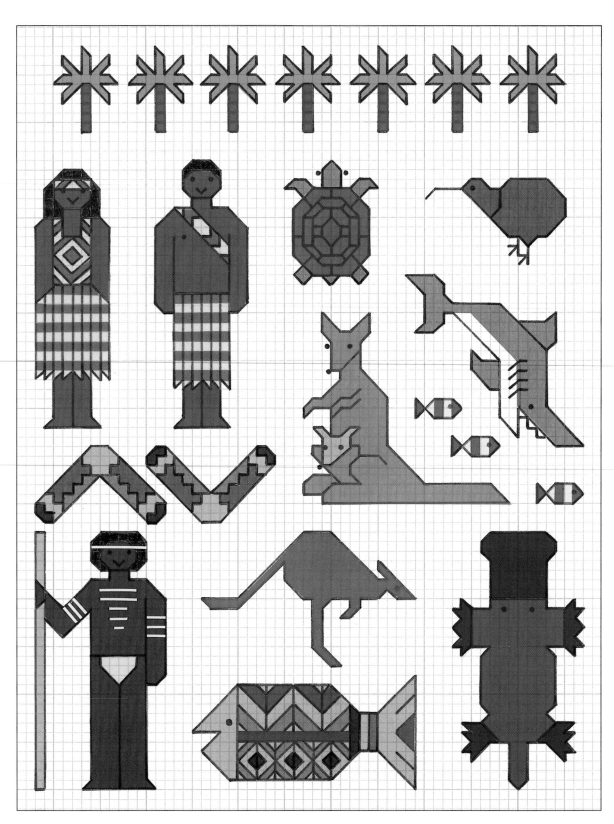

Australia

✠ Designs on Display ✠

Favourite designs have been worked on small pieces of fabric and have then been mounted into a display case. Cases such as this one normally house thimbles or other miniature collections, and are readily available in many shapes and sizes. Children enjoy helping with a project like this, as designs can be chosen that suit their abilities and pieces are small enough to be completed before interest wanes.

Plate 25 ▷

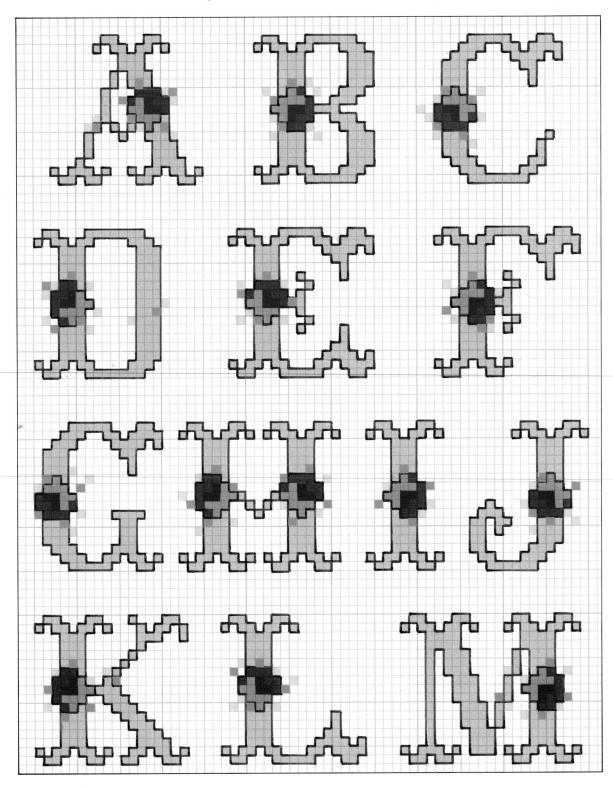

Take a single initial to personalise a keepsake, or spell
out names and messages using this floral alphabet.

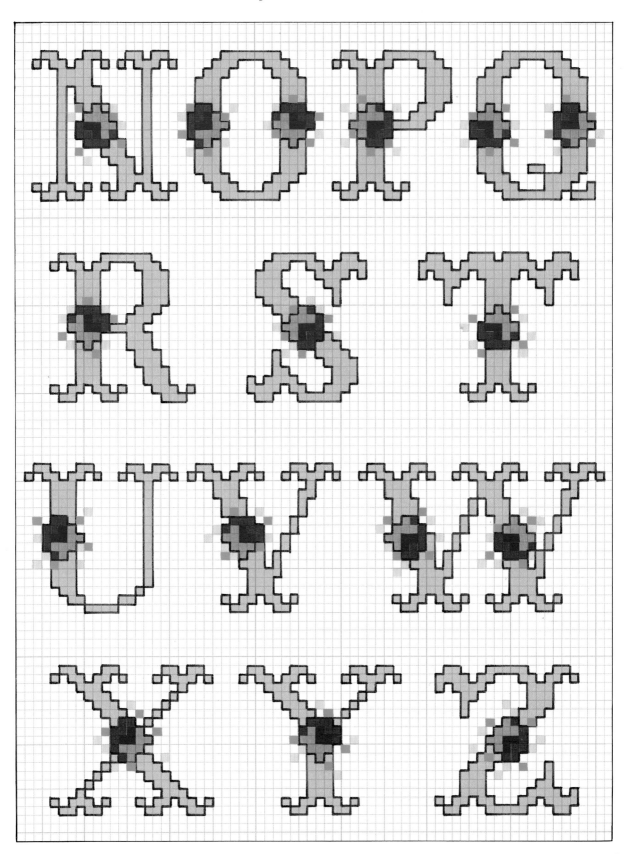

Fig 15

116

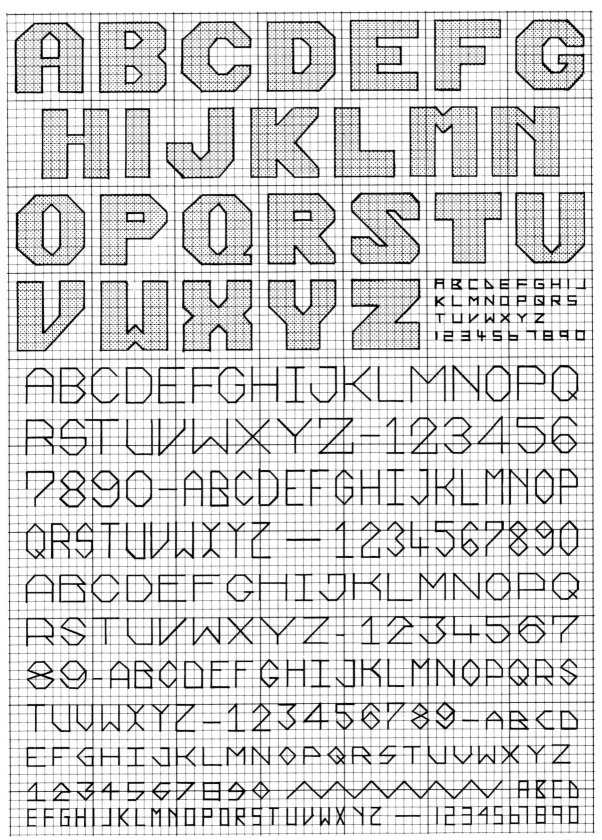

Fig 16

Stitching the Designs

FABRICS

First, you will need some evenweave or Aida fabric. There are many to choose from and it is very important to know the count of any fabric as this will determine the ultimate finished size of the design worked on it. The count given is the number of threads to 1in (2.5cm) on an evenweave fabric, or blocks to 1in (2.5cm) in the case of Aida. A 36-count evenweave fabric will produce 18 cross stitches to 1in (2.5cm) as the stitch is worked over two threads (see Fig 17). An 18-count Aida fabric will produce 18 cross stitches to 1in (2.5cm) as the stitch is worked over one block (see Fig 18).

Choose a fabric which does not strain your eyesight. Do not be put off because the photographed samples seem to be worked on very fine fabric. If you do not mind a larger result, a coarser fabric will make the work easier to see and still produce exactly the same design, but check that the finished work will fit the mount that you intend to use.

To do this, count the number of squares on your design both vertically and horizontally. Divide these numbers by the number of stitches produced per inch (centimetre) of your chosen fabric and you will know the size of the finished, stitched design. For example, if a chart measuring 100 squares by 50 squares is worked onto a fabric which produces 10 cross stitches to 1in (2.5cm), the finished embroidery will measure 10in (25cm) by 5in (12.5cm). Make this calculation before buying a piece of fabric to ensure that you buy enough to complete your design and thus avoid disappointment.

Aida fabrics are ideal for patterns which contain no three-quarter stitches, but with patience a hole can be pierced in the centre of the blocks to accommodate the stitch (see Fig 22). This problem can also be overcome by using a fine Aida and by working over two blocks instead of one (see Fig 23). This not only provides a central hole, but is a useful tip for people who wish to use the three-quarter stitch but whose eyesight cannot cope with an evenweave fabric. An 18-count Aida fabric will then produce 9 cross stitches to 1in (2.5cm). An example of this technique can be seen in the jampot cover (Plate 11).

The following fabrics were used in the worked samples shown in this book.

ZWEIGART RUSTICO – 18-count Aida, Flora Frame (Plate 7).

ZWEIGART DAMASK HARDANGER – 22-count evenweave, Religious Life (Plate 17).

ZWEIGART ANNABELLE – 28-count evenweave, World Map (Plate 20).

ZWEIGART AIDA (various counts) – pincushion (Plate 8), small sachet (Plate 8), pillow (Plate 7), work in progress (Plate 26).

ZWEIGART OSLO – 22-count evenweave, barn frame (Plate 11).

ZWEIGART EDINBOROUGH – 36-count evenweave, brooch (Plate 8). The thimble (Plate 8) was worked using one strand over one thread to get such a tiny result.

ZWEIGART SHONA DAMASK – 14-count Aida, pillow (Plate 22).

FRAMECRAFT JAR LACY – 18-count Aida, jampot cover (Plate 11).

INGLESTONE LINEN BAND WITH COLOURED EDGE – 28-count evenweave, honeysuckle bookmark (Plate 8). Matching tassels available.

INGLESTONE EYELET LINEN BAND – 28-count evenweave, cake frill (Plate 11).

ZWEIGART LINDA – 27-count evenweave, was used for all other designs in the book.

Buy or cut a piece of fabric large enough to accommodate your finished design, remembering to leave a good margin all round for turnings when mounting or framing. Oversew the edges of the fabric to prevent fraying. Find the centre of the fabric by folding it into four and mark this point temporarily with a pin. If the central stitch of your design is placed at this point, your work will be centred onto the fabric. Mount the fabric into an embroidery hoop large enough to contain the whole design, or mount it onto a suitably sized embroidery frame (Plate 26).

THREADS

All the designs in this book have been worked using stranded cotton. Both DMC and Anchor Mouline Stranded cottons are readily available in a vast variety of shades. On a fine fabric with 13 to 17 cross stitches

Plate 26 Embroidery materials ▷

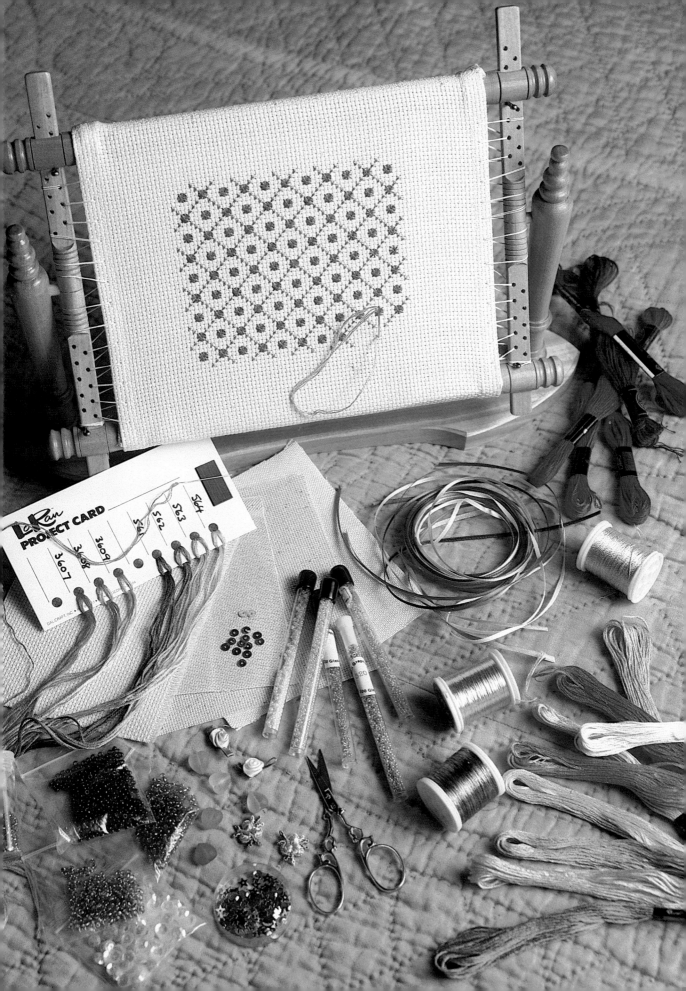

to 1in (2.5cm) use two strands of cotton for cross stitch and one strand for back stitch. On a coarser fabric with 9 to 12 stitches to 1in (2.5cm) use three strands of cotton for cross stitch and one or two strands for back stitch. Experiment on spare fabric to check that your chosen number of strands is giving good coverage of the fabric.

For extra glitter, occasional use has been made of DMC Fil d'Or (gold) and DMC Fil d'Argent (silver). Multi-coloured metallic Madeira threads add sparkle to mermaids' tails (Plates 18 and 20), where the basic cross stitches have been over-stitched by a single strand of metallic thread.

SEQUINS AND BEADS

Straight stitches are used to attach sequins to the fabric (Plates 20, 24 and 26). For neatest results, try to organise the stitching so that the needle always goes down through the hole in the sequin into the fabric.

The edible looking blackberries on the bramble border (Plate 15) were worked using beads rather than French knots. Thread a bead onto your cotton, and stitch it to the fabric using the first diagonal stitch of the full cross stitch. Keep all stitches slanting in the same direction to ensure that the beads lie in neat lines.

NEEDLES AND SCISSORS

Use a blunt tapestry needle for cross stitching. The size you use should be suitable for the fabric you are working on. It should slip easily through the holes in the fabric without enlarging or distorting them. Fine needles for use on fine fabrics have a high number on the packet (26), coarser needles have lower numbers.

Embroidery scissors must have very fine points and must be kept sharp. Avoid cutting anything other than embroidery thread with them. If you hang them around your neck on a ribbon they will always be at hand.

STITCHES

Full Cross Stitch

A full square on the chart indicates the use of a full cross stitch. The stitch is formed by a first diagonal stitch, which is then covered with another diagonal stitch in the opposite direction (Figs 17, 18, 19).

When working rows of full cross stitches, bring the needle out at the left-hand side of the row and work a row of half crosses. Return, making the complete

Fig 17 A full cross stitch worked over two threads on evenweave fabric

Fig 18 A full cross stitch worked over one block on Aida fabric

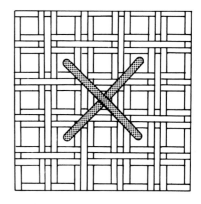

Fig 19 A full cross stitch worked over two blocks on Aida fabric

crosses, working from right to left and using the same holes as before (Fig 20). All stitches interlock, sharing holes with their neighbours unless they are single stitches worked on their own.

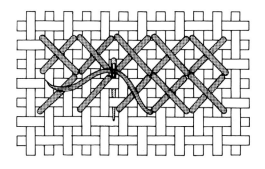

Fig 20 Working lines of full cross stitches

Three-Quarter Cross Stitch

A right-angled triangle on the chart indicates the use of this stitch. The first half of the cross stitch is worked in the usual way, but the second 'quarter' stitch is

Fig 21 Four examples of three-quarter cross stitch worked on evenweave fabric

Fig 22 A three-quarter cross stitch worked over one block on Aida fabric

brought across and down into the central hole (Fig 21). If working on Aida the quarter stitch must be worked into the centre of the block (Fig 22). If working over two blocks of Aida proceed as in Fig 23. Where the chart indicates the use of two three-quarter stitches together, these are worked using the same central hole and occupying the space of one full cross stitch (Fig 24).

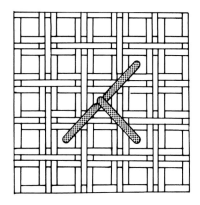

Fig 23 A three-quarter cross stitch worked over two blocks on Aida fabric

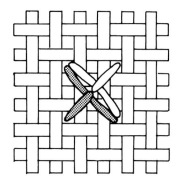

Fig 24 Two three-quarter cross stitches sewn back to back, occupying the space of one full cross stitch

Back Stitch (Fig 25, overleaf)

The use of back stitch is indicated on your chart by a solid line. Back stitch is worked around and sometimes over the finished cross stitch to give definition and detail to the work. As a general rule, outline a pale colour with a deeper tone of the same colour if you have it. Otherwise use a grey, or even black on very dark colours. Back stitch is also used for lettering.

Bring the needle out at 1 and in at 2. Bring it out again at 3 and in at 4. Continue this sequence in the direction indicated by the chart.

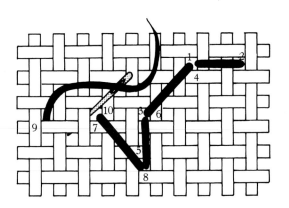

Fig 25 Back stitch

French Knots (Figs 26a & 26b)

The use of this stitch will be indicated by a dot on your chart. French knots are invaluable for embroidering eyes, buttons, tiny flowers etc onto your cross stitch.

Fig 26a Working a French knot   Fig 26b Finished knot

Bring the needle out one thread to the right of where you want the knot to lie. Slip the needle twice under the thread so that the twists lie snugly around the needle. Without allowing the thread to untwist, insert the needle back into the fabric, one thread to the left of where you started. Pull the thread through to the back and the knot is completed. For larger knots use more strands of thread or a thicker needle.

TIPS

* Press any stubborn creases out of your fabric before you start to stitch.
* For best results the full cross stitches should be worked with all the top stitches lying in the same direction.
* Avoid carrying thread across the back of bare fabric. A ghostly trail will be visible when the work is mounted. It is, however, acceptable to run thread from one area to another through the back of existing stitches, taking care not to distort them.
* When starting and finishing a thread, avoid using knots. These give a lumpy appearance to the work when it is mounted. Loose ends should be woven securely into the back of existing stitches. Trim all ends of thread very close to the fabric or they will be visible when the work is mounted.
* It is very disheartening to have to unpick and re-work, so count the stitches carefully as you proceed and check your work regularly against the chart.
* Allow the needle to dangle upside down from the work frequently to remove any twists from the thread. Threads give better coverage when lying flat.
* Avoid soiling your work by keeping it covered when you are not stitching. Protect it from hazards such as cups of tea, inquisitive cats and small children who have just eaten a chocolate biscuit.

Finishing Touches

When you have finished your work, check it carefully for mistakes, missed stitches, loose ends on the back and other horrors.

PRESSING YOUR EMBROIDERY

It is still possible to ruin your work at this stage by pressing it incorrectly. Stitches can be flattened so that the work looks lifeless. To avoid this, lay a fluffy, white, terry towel on a flat surface. Place your work face down on the towel and cover it with a thin, white, cotton cloth. Press gently with a warm iron to remove all creases in the fabric. The stitches will sink into the pile of the towel and will not be flattened at all. When the work is turned over it will have a pleasing embossed appearance.

FRAMING

Any embroidery which is to be placed in a frame is best taken to a reputable framer. A good framer will give your work the professional finishing touch it deserves. My framer will even mount work into brooches, hair brushes, jar lids, Flora Frames, tennis racquets, display cases and so on.

Ask to have the work mounted onto acid-free card to avoid unsightly brown spots (foxing) which can develop later. All my framed work is finished with clear glass which is not allowed to come into contact with the stitches, to avoid flattening them. This is achieved by using an acid-free mount, or by placing fine strips of acid-free card around the edges where the overlap of the frame will hide them from view.

To prevent fading, avoid hanging your embroidery in full sunlight.

To frame embroidery into a tennis racquet (Plate 13), remove the strings carefully and ask your local joiner to cut a rebate into the back of it before presenting it to your framer.

MOUNTING GREETINGS CARDS

The mounting of greetings cards can be tackled at home. Ready-made card mounts are available in many shapes, sizes and colours. It is best to check that the design you are planning will fit the mount that you intend to use. If the design is too large you can usually solve the problem by working on a finer fabric.

Embroidery is mounted into the card using double-sided sticky tape. Place the double-sided sticky tape around the window on the inside of the card and around the edges on section (a) (Fig 27). Trim your work to fit the card. Lay your work face up on a flat surface. Remove the backing strips from the sticky tape on section (b). With the outside of the card facing you, stick the window around your embroidery, making sure that it is straight. A squirt of an adhesive such as Spray-Mount on section (a) will give the embroidery a sticky surface to cling to; without it the embroidery has a tendency to ripple. Remove the backing from the sticky tape on section (a) and fold section (a) over section (b). This will glue the two sections together and hide the back of the embroidery. Write your message on section (c). Trim your card with ribbon, lace or braid, as desired.

The 'Bon Voyage' luggage label (Plate 11) can be made by cutting the mount yourself or by buying two luggage labels. Cut a window in one and glue the two together, positioning the embroidery between the two labels and behind the window.

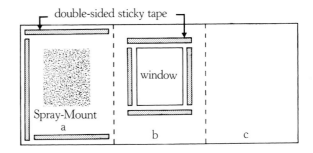

Fig 27 Mounting work into a card

COVERING A PHOTOGRAPH ALBUM

To cover a photograph album (Plate 12), first make sure that you have chosen a suitable album. Some flip-up albums are not suitable for this treatment, as the fabric pockets prevent the photos from flipping up. A good photographic shop will stock albums which have pages onto which the photographs are mounted and this is the kind used here.

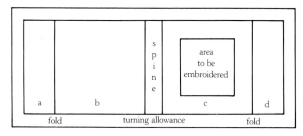

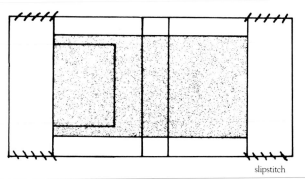

Fig 28 Layout of fabric to be cut for a photograph album cover (right side)

Fig 29 The finished cover (wrong side)

Fold your fabric around your album, then cut enough fabric to allow for turnings and two end pockets. Tack the fold lines and make a note of which section is to be embroidered (Fig 28). When the embroidery is complete, hemstitch the turnings on the inside of the cover. Wrong sides together, fold section (a) over section (b) and slipstitch as shown, to form a pocket. Repeat with the other end, fold section (d) over section (c) and slipstitch to form another pocket (Fig 29). Remove all tacking thread. Slip the album cover into the two end pockets and smooth the cover into place.

BOOKMARKS

To make a bookmark, neaten the top and the bottom of the work with a small hem. On the wrong side, stitch (a) to (b) to form a point. If you wish to hide the back of the stitching, line the bookmark with ribbon or thin felt. Finish by adding a tassel to the point (Fig 30).

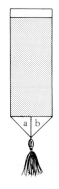

Fig 30 Making up a bookmark

PILLOWS AND SACHETS

When making small pillows or sachets, cut a piece of backing fabric to fit the finished work. Place the two pieces of fabric right sides together and sew around the edge, leaving a gap for turning. Trim away excess fabric and clip curves. Turn right side out, stuff with your chosen filling and slipstitch the opening closed. Finally trim with lace, ribbon, beads, or whatever takes your fancy.

READY-MADE MOUNTS

If you buy a mount such as a porcelain pot, pincushion base, dressing table set etc, the manufacturers' instructions will tell you how to proceed, or you could always smile sweetly at your framer.

Further Reading

Picture It in Cross Stitch Jo Verso
(David & Charles, 1988)
Very detailed instructions on designing and stitching. A Pattern Library is included which contains many more designs, all of which can be used in conjunction with this book. Projects include family, birth and wedding samplers, family trees and much more.

Cross Stitch Cards and Keepsakes Jo Verso
(David & Charles, 1990)
Small projects; greetings cards and keepsakes for most occasions. All the major festivals throughout the year are catered for, as are the celebrations in life. Colour keys for both DMC and Anchor threads are provided for each design, together with detailed instructions on mounting and finishing projects. All designs can be used in conjunction with those in this book.

Cross Stitch Castles and Cottages Jane Greenoff
(David & Charles, 1989)

Traditional Samplers Sarah Don
(David & Charles, 1986)

Samplers Averil Colby (Batsford, 1964)

Making Samplers Jutta Lammer
(Sterling Publishing Co Inc, 1984)

Needlepoint Samplers Felicity Lewis (Cassell, 1981)

Embroidery Motifs from Dutch Samplers
Albarta Meulenbelt-Nieuwburg (Batsford, 1974)

Samplers Ann Sebba (Weidenfield & Nicolson, 1979)

Flags Collins Gem Guide (Collins, 1986)

Acknowledgements

I owe an enormous debt of gratitude to the valiant team of stitchers who worked so willingly and so expertly to get this book produced on time. Many thanks, therefore, to Gill Broad, Carol Burr, Eileen Callender, Hazel Evans, Ros Foster, Margaret Jones, Sandra Kedzlie, Elizabeth Lovesey, Edna McCready, Sue Moir, Sue Moore, Sylvia Morgan, Penny Peberdy, Sylvia Read, Pam Rivers, Elizabeth Smith, Linda Smith, Jean Sutton, Amy Verso, Nancy Verso, Irene Vincent and Jenny Way.

Many thanks to Sarah Widdicombe and Brenda Morrison at David & Charles for their help and contributions to the production of this book. A big thank you to Di Lewis for her photographs; seeing the transparencies as they arrived was always a delight. Thank you to Alan Duns who photographed Plate 20.

My thanks to the staff at Kenilworth Library, who never failed to find me the illustration I needed, and to John Edwards for his help and support.

I am indebted to Tony Foster at Warwick Studios, 206-208 Emscote Road, Warwick CV34 5QT, tel (0926) 494714, for his expert framing. Not once has he been stumped by any of my more unusual requests. Thank you also to Wendy for her patience, helpfulness and efficiency.

When contacting suppliers by post for catalogues or other information, please always enclose a SAE. If you telephone them, they will be able to tell you if there is a charge for their price list or catalogue.

I am grateful to the following suppliers for their generous assistance in the production of this book:

Cara Ackerman at DMC Creative World Ltd, Pullman Road, Wigston, Leicestershire LE8 2DY, tel (0533) 811040 (all Zweigart fabrics, DMC stranded cottons, Gothic 9½in (24cm) frame (Plate 17), tapestry needles, greetings card mounts and embroidery sundries).

Mike Grey at Framecraft Miniatures Ltd, 148/150 High Street, Aston, Birmingham B6 4US, tel (021) 3594442 (thimble, brooch, porcelain pots, dressing table set, circular frame on an easel (Plate 8), Jar Lacy and CraftaCards (Plate 11)). Framecraft products are also supplied by:

>   Anne Brinkley Designs Inc, 21 Ransom
>   Road, Newton Centre, Mass. 02159 USA.
>   Ireland Needlecraft, 16 Mavron Street,
>   Ashwood 3147 Australia.

Jim Clark at Coats Leisure Crafts Group Ltd, 39 Durham Street, Glasgow G41 1BS, tel (041) 4275311 (Anchor Mouline Stranded Cottons).

Jane Greenoff, The Inglestone Collection, Milton Place, Fairford, Gloucestershire GL7 4HR, tel (0285) 712778 (evenweave linen bands with coloured edges and matching tassels, evenweave eyelet linen bands).

Offray Ribbon Ltd, Ashbury Road, Roscrea, Co Tipperary, Ireland (ribbon).

Lawrance and Lowings, Lea Valley Trading Estate, Angel Road, Edmonton, London N18 3HN, tel (081) 8039708 (Lilliput embroidery frame – Plate 26).

Niz Jivraj at Euro Graphics (Wembley), 197 East Lane, North Wembley, Middlesex HA9 3NG, tel (081) 9083755 (graph paper by mail order).

R & P Sperr, S & A Frames, 12 Humber Street, Cleethorpes, South Humberside DN35 8NN, tel (0472) 697772 (barn frame and horseshoe frame – Plate 11).

Colin Gordon, Fleeting Image, 10 Greendale Court, Honley, Huddersfield, West Yorkshire HD7 2JW, tel (0484) 666401 (Heirloom Victorian Frame and matching mount – Plate 10).

Beryl Lee at Artisan, 19-21 High Street, Pinner, Middlesex HA5 5PJ, tel (081) 8660327 (tracing graph paper, Easy Grid, pincushion base (Plate 8) and needlecraft supplies).

Roger Massey at Artistic Basic Designs Limited, The Estate Office, Hill Farm House, Hittisleigh, Exeter, Devon EX6 6LQ, tel (0647) 24613 (Flora Frame – Plate 7).

Découpage Designs, Cherry Tree House, 14 Rostrop Road, Nocton, Lincolnshire LN4 2BT, tel (0526) 22650 (frame – Plate 14).

The Campden Needlecraft Centre, High Street, Chipping Campden, Gloucestershire GL55 6AG, tel (0386) 840583 (ribbon and needlework supplies).

The Voirrey Embroidery Centre, Brimstage Hall, Brimstage, Wirrall L63 6JA, tel (051) 3423514 (needlecraft supplies).

Craft Creations Ltd, Unit 6, Harpers Yard, Ruskin Road, Tottenham, London N17 8NE, tel (081) 8852655 (greetings card mounts).

D T Wright, Herald Way, Binley Industrial Estate, Coventry, Warwickshire CV3 2RQ, tel (0203) 341055, who cut the rebate in the tennis racquet (Plate 13).

Mary Burgess at Rod Waspe Ltd, 1 Millar Court, Station Road, Kenilworth, Warwickshire CV8 1JJ, tel (0926) 59774, (stationery and graphics supplies).

✤ Acknowledgements ✤

Stuart Gordon at Ursa Minor, Cilgeraint House, St Ann's, Bethesda, Gwynedd LL57 4AX, tel (0248) 600195 (miniature pottery bears – Plate 25).

Janet Coles Beads, Perdiswell Cottage, Bilford Road, Worcester WR8 8QA, tel (0905) 755888 (8/0 oily black blue beads for blackberries – Plates 15 & 26, heart shaped beads – Plates 11 & 26).

Carole Morris at Spangles, 1 Casburn Lane, Burwell, Cambs CB5 0ED, tel (0638) 742024 (8/0 red, pink and green beads for blackberries – Plates 15 & 26).

My chart for the map of the world (Plate 20), in black & white with a colour key for both DMC and Anchor stranded cottons, complete with full instructions, is available from the Inglestone Collection, Milton Place, Fairford, Gloucestershire GL7 4HR, tel (0285) 712778. Please enclose a SAE with all enquiries.

Index

Page numbers in *italics* indicate illlustrations